Small Wonders

Reviews and Commentary

2002-2003

Jessie Thorpe

MOUNTAIN LAKE PRESS
Mountain Lake Park, Maryland

Author's note:
In the parenthetical details to the books reviewed in this collection, I have referenced their original editions and most frequently in hardcover. Since that time, and in most cases, the hardcovers have gone out of print but alternative editions have emerged, including paperback, ebook and audio versions, so all of the titles should remain available to interested readers.

Small Wonders
Reviews and Commentary
By Jessie Thorpe

Reprinted by permission
Original content copyright © United Press International
New content copyright © 2018 Jessie Thorpe
All Rights Reserved

ISBN: 978-1-959307-22-8

Published in the United States of America
By Mountain Lake Press

Printed in the United States of America

I dedicate this book to my mother
Susan Lloyd Dent
With great love and gratitude

Contents

INTRODUCTION ... 6
BOOK REVIEWS ... 10
Audacious 'Rollow Sisters' ... 10
Dreaming of the 'Wolf Girl' ... 12
A defiant 'Young Woman' ... 15
It really is a 'Small Wonder' ... 17
Thank you, 'Jesus' ... 20
On the 'Roads' again ... 22
'Red Sky' is riveting ... 25
A sweet slice of 'Pie' ... 28
Please open 'The God File' ... 31
'Metal' is pure grade ... 33
The 'Greatest' Lincoln ... 36
Deep thoughts of 'Command' ... 39
A real 'Nowhere Man' ... 42
Women scorned writing 'Letters' ... 46
Dining on 'Lobster' ... 48
Mixed 'Blessings' ... 52
An artful 'Forgery' ... 55
An unforgettable 'Mentor' ... 59
A hard working 'Manifesto' ... 61
Not 'Crazed' after all ... 65
Won't Quite 'Take You There' ... 68
Don't be a 'Stranger' ... 71

Travel as 'Art'	74
Odyssey from 'East' to 'West'	77
A lingering 'Afterglow'	82
A concise 'Churchill'	85
Showing us 'How to Be Alone'	88
A divine 'Emperor'	91
A gripping 'Panda' chase	94
'Leonardo' meets computer	98
Pearls among 'Pinstripes'	101
'Food' for thought	105
'Extremely Happy' company	108
'Book Club' a must-read	111
Take the 'Power' trip	114
A well-rounded 'Crescent'	117
A 'Devil' with few details	120
No 'Shortcuts' indeed	123
A 'Wife' for all seasons	127
A 'Walk' worth taking	130
The shocking secrets of 'Gender Talk'	132
A dazzling 'Funeral'	135
Falling from the 'Heights'	138
Walking 'Hallowed Ground'	141
Happily recalling 'All That'	144
Heroic and human 'John Paul Jones'	148
James Wood, critic, tries a novel. Pity.	151

Go fly a kite, Mr. Franklin 154
Food writer becomes 'Ambulance Girl' 158
'Candy' is dandy 161
What some people do 'in the Name of God' 164
Steve Martin is a 'Pleasure' 169
'Intelligence' does not always win 172
FILM REVIEWS 175
Those secrets of the 'Ya-Ya Sisterhood' 175
Where was Seabiscuit? 178
'Sun' goes under a cloud 181
'Sylvia' alive on screen 186
COMMENTARY 191
The National Book Festival: Literacy revived 191
Books for Baghdad 194
A fond new gaze at Anne Frank 198
Dedicated to the ones she loves 202
This year's Book Festival a best-seller 206
Religion still propels best-sellers 209
PUBLISHER'S NOTE: 212

INTRODUCTION

You will never meet my marvelous mother. Mary Hatch Bailey in the film "It's a Wonderful Life" reminds me of her. Like Mary, with her upswept hair and braid, Mom was a busy and cheerful woman who made her home the place you wanted to be. Not to demean the delightful Clarence Oddbody, but I quietly believe Mary is the true angel in the story.

Among her other outstanding qualities, my mother filled her children's lives with reading. She read to us constantly. Almost weekly, she took us to the library and let us putter around and check out as many volumes as allowed. Those early scents and texture and deliciousness of books are treasured memories. Now, I honestly do not know how I would get on in life without them.

A favorite poem of mine is Strickland Gillian's "The Reading Mother," which ends:

> *You may have tangible wealth untold*
> *Caskets of jewels and coffers of gold.*
> *Richer than I you can never be –*
> *I had a Mother who read to me.*

At Christmas every year, we children each received at least two new books. Bliss for me was sneaking off to park myself by a heat register (it was always freezing in Michigan on Christmas Day) and cuddling up in warmth to enjoy a new adventure. Mom understood the comfort and security a child feels when reading. She seldom interrupted any of us when we were thus engaged.

A lifetime of reading expands one's mind in exciting ways. Starting young as I did, and not being restricted in my choices, I let one book lead me to another, and another. In my youth, I loved simple biographies of great Americans. Reading about Abraham Lincoln led me to books on the Civil War and then to U.S. Grant, to John Wilkes Booth and so on. Reading a single Jane Austen novel when I was 12 drove me to devour all of her novels during one summer. I did not even know they were great literature; I just loved them.

I'm happy to have a book lead me anywhere.

So it seemed like a dream come true when, in the summer of 2002, United Press International offered me the opportunity to write reviews and commentary for a desk called Life and Art. For various reasons, I had not worked at a paid position in quite a while and feared my writing skills had grown a bit rusty to use serving a major news organization. Nevertheless, I accepted and soon found, in mid-life, new enjoyment and challenge. Even though my first efforts were wobbly, I quickly got the hang of what was required and learned to file my columns like a pro.

Of great help were the two editors who accepted every piece I sent them, rarely changed a word and never assigned me a topic. I was free to choose subjects that interested me at the time – mostly books and films. Turned out I loved the discipline of meeting deadlines. Because I held no particular credentials – not being an academic or specialist of any kind – I chose to write as if to a friend. The approach allowed me to connect with others, many others, readers I would never meet. Although I was never formally syndicated, I became fascinated seeing how many news outlets picked up my columns from UPI. They included such widely separated places as the Cayman Islands and Sacramento and Fresno, California.

Eventually – much too soon, alas – UPI management decided to stop covering cultural topics in favor of national security and health issues. Given what was happening in the country at the time, that was probably a sensible move. I went on to another job that gave me greater remuneration but not nearly as much fun. I felt no regrets; yet the desire to retain something of that time – the excitement, the pressure and collegial sharing – lingered in me.

When my current publisher/partner asked me to revisit my old columns with an eye toward collecting them in a book, I at first felt reluctant. One of my mother's many endearing philosophical expressions popped into my mind: "Love the moment; let it pass." I employ the phrase a lot, and it seemed to fit that particular moment. Something I had loved was long over, so let it be. I truly do not like to dwell in the past. I find it difficult to see old photos of myself, for instance. My reaction is always either that I used to look better, or I look freaky with a terrible outfit and awkward hairstyle.

Yet, honestly, I was intrigued. With mixed feelings, I began to read over the work. Many moments passed in "God, what was I thinking?" agony. I have always been and remain a harsh critic of my writing.

Then something unexpected happened. I began to remember the happiness of those days, the joy of receiving a letter or email from an author whose work I had reviewed praising that review because I really "got" his or her novel.

Something else happened as I continued reading my words. The post-9/11 aftermath returned to mind, how the country was still reeling from that great tragedy. I noticed in some of my columns subtexts tinted with such feelings. Without consciously presuming to comment on foreign policy or military tactics, I often touched on those topics when critiquing fictional or biographical works.

I was reminded how books connect us in many ways -- to ideas, to people, to life. I think that is why I can never get enough of exploring the world through the minds of others. Remembering the friends and connections so nourishing back then, I decided to go ahead and publish this collection. I could have revised and annotated some of the pieces, but I think their value might be greater in leaving the work as it was presented at the time. Are some of the reviews dated? Maybe. But honest writing is timeless, and so I send this book along for old and, perhaps, new friends.

Jessie Thorpe
November 2018

BOOK REVIEWS

Audacious 'Rollow Sisters'
First published June 19, 2002

One has to admire an author who sets his first novel in rural Nebraska.

That landscape was put on the literary map a century ago by Willa Cather, and she has pretty much dominated the territory ever since. Yet, as its narrative both sweet and audacious unfolds, *The Phantom Limbs of the Rollow Sisters* encroaches on Cather's pinnacle just a bit.

The plight of the sisters begins like a fairy tale. Schaffert quickly sketches two young women opposite in appearance and personality. One is fair and round, one is dark with a pointy chin, and together they need to be set free.

But rather than waiting to be rescued, these girls are up to the task of slaying dragons from their weird childhood on their own.

We meet Mabel and Lily at 21 and 18, living in the country near Bonnevilla, Nebraska (pop. 2,900), in a ramshackle house filled with old junk. They are so alone out there that Lily feels "claustrophobic" in the emptiness.

The girls' mother, Fiona, fled to Mexico 10 years previously after their father Eddy committed suicide. The circumstances of that event are clouded in mystery and lies. Their grandmother hung around, in vague absentee fashion, until Lily finished high school and then escaped to a condo in Florida.

These young women have no blueprint for life. They know their parents from odds and ends, bits and pieces of broken furniture and ripped dresses. Lily and Mabel are never pitiable, just earnestly trying to figure out life with precious little help. They try to act adult, drinking cocktails and listening to their father's old records. Lily moves into an abandoned school bus out back and calls it her "apartment".

It seems that the descendants of pioneers who flocked to this land are all on their way out. Mabel – dark, thin, intense – wanders the back roads in her beaten pickup, filching relics from deserted churches and farmhouses to supply her antique business. Lily's blonde curls and plump, pretty figure suggest her capricious and wayward heart. She has no interest in Mabel's resourcefulness, although she does recognize "the beauty of poor neglected things."

One of these neglected things is Jordan, an oddly appealing manicurist and singer who loves Lily and likes Mabel a lot. He wants to drive Lily to Mexico to search for her mother. Somewhat improbably for a wannabe hero, he owns a '56 Packard that once belonged to Charles Starkweather, the sinister serial killer who, decades before, had rampaged around the state, terrorizing the entire population. But Lily provides for the getaway herself and they take off in a partially stolen Chevrolet Monte Carlo. Lily discards Jordan in Las Vegas and completes her pilgrimage alone, convinced that she will discover truth from her mother and answers to questions she longs to ask.

Mabel, left behind, embarks on a different journey. Grappling with her ghostly burdens, she hooks up with a fraud of sorts, a faker who counterfeits messages from the dead. At last, she rids the house of its rubbish and hauls the mess to the dump.

Lily returns, having learned a secret about her parents that she wisely decides to keep to herself. Mabel has changed also. She has acquired courage to choose what to keep and value.

There's a nice scene at the end with the sisters sitting on the roof, sipping sherry from vineyards tended by their mother. Although neither one has ended up with Prince Charming, they are beginning to shape lives of their own.

I want to know what becomes of these brave and funny sisters.

The descriptive gifts of the author are great. His directions are so precise that when I finished his lovely book, I made a mental note that if I'm ever driving in that neck of the woods, I should turn off I-80 onto Route 34 and look for Mabel's sign: "Antiques 2 MI." And if I go a bit farther, I just might see the weathered farmhouse with a yellow school bus rusting in the yard.

(*The Phantom Limbs of the Rollow Sisters* by Timothy Schaffert. Blue Hen Books/Penguin Putnam, 2002. 228 pages)

Dreaming of the 'Wolf Girl'
June 26, 2002

Here is a useful technique for reading *La Tour Dreams of the Wolf Girl* by David Huddle. Imagine you are back in college, sitting in a darkened lecture hall. The art history professor flashes slides on a screen, one after another, drawing your eye to certain details in the paintings before rapidly moving on. The pictures don't seem to connect in any way.

The story begins with a flash on Suzanne Yarborough, growing up poor in the mountains of Virginia. After forming an unusual bond with a mute classmate, who communicates by drawing on his notebook, she treats him in a heartless manner.

Another picture. Jack Nelson, a young man of privilege, helps a disturbed girl at a summer camp. Although he is proud of his perceptions and generosity of spirit, the girl ultimately rejects him.

We are shown a slide of the village of Luneville in 17th-century France. The aging but powerful resident artist, Georges de La Tour, swaggers through town with his nasty dogs, annoying and despising the peasants. He wants Vivienne Lavalette, the shoemaker's daughter, to pose for him, and he is willing to pay for her.

The novel moves back and forth in time and place. Jack and Suzanne meet and marry. Suzanne is an art historian. Jack is "the public relations genius of the state of Vermont" and has an affair with a teacher in Suzanne's department. Suzanne dedicates her career to becoming an expert on Georges de La Tour.

La Tour makes a discovery while painting Vivienne. She possesses the "wolf shoulder," a pelt of silky dark hair on her spine, positioned in such a way that she is innocent of its existence. Horrified and fascinated, the artist makes her aware of it and thus changes her nature.

Huddle tells his story by interweaving themes and imagery, forcefully unifying his tale. Suzanne poses nude for a college professor. Vivienne never poses nude for La Tour but allows him to sense her body when he is old and blind and no longer painting. La Tour asks questions of Vivienne as she poses hour after hour ,and she answers him with lies. Jack "tells the same lie over and over" in both his professional and personal life. Suzanne looks down on her inferior students. La Tour disdains the villagers.

The characters repeatedly behave in cruel and hurtful ways to one another. Yet they are not despicable. There is a kind of calm and stirring energy throughout the book. The people do what they must to create their lives.

Creation is at the heart of this story. The author asks us to ponder the meaning of truth and humanity in art. Does it matter if a picture factually represents its subject? Must an artist be a kind or "nice guy" to create inspired work?

Did La Tour exist as Huddle describes him, ending his life alone, ancient and blind, feeding off a pliant girl? I don't think so. A glance at his biography reveals he died at 59, depressed from his wife's death a few weeks previously and with nine of his ten children still living.

The artist in the novel is Huddle's own compelling interpretation, wonderfully drawn and unsentimental. He portrays La Tour as a fierce old man, kicking up dust and scaring people. The pictures and words ring true.

Joseph Conrad famously said that the business of the novelist is to make us see. Without lecturing, David Huddle has made us see the influence of art in our lives. Novels that use real artists as main characters have practically become a genre by themselves. I would say *Wolf Girl* is a worthy contender in this form. Huddle's use of detail to reflect and interpret emotion is masterful.

One caution. If you are a reader who likes linear stories with a definite beginning, middle and end, do not choose *La Tour Dreams of the Wolf Girl*. This novel is all middle.

I happen to like middle.

(*La Tour Dreams of the Wolf Girl* by David Huddle. Houghton Mifflin, 2002. 196 pages)

A defiant 'Young Woman'
July 5, 2002

In addition to her coursework in the MFA Creative Writing program at the University of Washington in Seattle, Sandi Sonnenfeld also worked as a copy editor, took dance classes and performed an original composition, engaged in two romances, won a $5,000 literary prize and wrote regularly in a journal. The latter became *This Is How I Speak: The Diary of a Young Woman*.

Sonnenfeld's sojourn took place 15 years ago when she was turning 25. Now that she is approaching 40, she brings this work to market "as is," as they say in the real estate business.

In the introduction, she states that aside from minor changes, she has left her entries exactly as they were so as not to "denigrate the thoughts and feelings of a twenty-four-year-old American woman artist struggling to make sense of herself in a world that largely neither admires artists nor women."

That is quite a statement and, I would say, debatable. Yet it sets the tone of the book, protective and defiant with flaming self-regard.

Sonnenfeld begins with a laundry list of her fears – dogs, snakes and hairy men – but her greatest fear is being ordinary. She seethes with ambition, with the need to stand out and be recognized as an artist. She is vastly jealous of the success of others.

It's easy to poke fun at an effort like this. Sonnenfeld rages at the nasty business of writing workshops which forces one to endure repeatedly the pain and humiliation of hearing one's manuscript ripped to shreds. Yet, with no irony or insight, she sits down one night after a frustrating dance audition to read through a stack of stories written by fellow students. She crosses out lines and entire sentences that she judges to be superfluous. "I am merciless," she writes, angrily. "It does not make me feel any better."

Sonnenfeld's clunky use of non-words such as "numerable" and "uncompassionate" made me cringe. Her constant references to her youth, to being on the "threshold of adulthood" at 25 made me wonder at what age she thinks adulthood begins.

It's best not to take the author too seriously. She tells us rather often that she is smart, pretty, talented and infinitely knowledgeable about literature. Her confident opinions on subjects from expatriate writers to the Vietnam War are scattered on every page. "The only way to stop war," she tells us seriously, "is for both fans and players to refuse to show up for the game." This is amusing stuff.

We also learn that she missed an entire undergraduate year at Mt. Holyoke because of depression, has unresolved anger toward her family and vests her teachers with enormous power over her sense of self-worth.

Reading between the lines, a portrait emerges of a conflicted woman/child who longs to be heard but tells people she wants to write with no words. She keeps playing with the idea of a totally silent character and writes: "Fiction is the only way I can find the words to the silence that is myself."

Yes, I thought, work on that silence!

Literary journals and diaries can provide fascinating glimpses into the life and sources behind great works. Often they are just gossipy good fun. The whining complaints of Tolstoy come to mind and also the chronicles of John Cheever, recording the exact hour of the day when he took his first drink.

Sonnenfeld has somehow jumped the gun. I think it's important to produce the work first before publishing your raw scribblings about process. Don't invite us into your studio to show off your paint pots and smudged brushes before you have put something real on the canvas.

Although Sonnenfeld has published numerous journalism pieces and stories in art magazines, this is her first book. It has taken so long because, as she says, agents and publishers have tried to convince her to turn this diary into fiction or memoir. What good advice! There are several vignettes here that I think might be fashioned into real art. One passage, for instance, about a creepy encounter with a former teacher who pours out his inner thoughts but must do it in the nude is great material.

This spirited author is determined to have life on her own terms, including having her book published in her own way. I hope she now has it out of her system and will take a mature look at these youthful words. Rich honest stories are waiting to be discovered in what is a very personal – but should have remained private – laboratory.

(*This Is How I Speak: The Diary of a Young Woman* by Sandi Sonnenfeld. Impassio Press, 2002. 168 pages)

It really is a 'Small Wonder'
July 15, 2002

Barbara Kingsolver's *Small Wonder* could not be more aptly titled. The essays in this wonderful collection are not small in meager or insignificant ways. They begin with Kingsolver describing some interesting slices of life, as if examining them under a microscope, and then expanding her view to take in the larger world.

"I'd like to speak of small wonders and the possibility of taking heart," the author says, and that is just what she proceeds to do. Kingsolver is best known for her novels, all of which explore human beings interacting with one other and the natural world, and trying to do their utmost for both. These essays are almost a continuation of the dialogue she sets up in her fiction, only now she speaks directly to the reader as she probes deeply into her own personal universe.

When you admire a writer, as I do this one, it's natural to be curious about her life. I have read that she lives in Tucson, Arizona, and on a farm in Appalachia. She also alludes to this in her fiction. For such a popular author, other facts have been elusive, however. She does not often do book tours, nor does she appear on talk shows. So the details in these pieces seem especially fascinating.

Kingsolver grows almost all the food her family eats. She does not watch television, which she calls "the one-eyed monster," nor do her two daughters. She loves this country with a passion second only to her fierce motherlove. I do not doubt that this woman passes many of her precious hours (she guards her minutes like the crown jewels) in radiant happiness. Try reading "Lily's Chickens" here and see if you don't agree.

She despairs over what we do to our children and agonizes over what is happening to this precious planet. Yet she states her opinions with intelligent concern for truth: We must stop gobbling up the world's resources, we must find more conserving ways to feed ourselves, we must use our time more wisely, we must not do "this killing thing."

I forgive the few places where her tone becomes strident and slightly preachy. Perhaps it is frustrating that she is unable to create a happy ending for the real world as she can in her novels.

I admire what she's trying to do here – taking risks by putting ideas on the page that are not exactly popular. Let's face it, who wants to be lectured about how much TV one watches? Yet she makes a good case that watching TV leaves one with a desperate sense that the entire world is exploding all the time.

With matter-of-fact pride, she relates that when a friend called and mentioned the death of JFK Jr., Kingsolver said she hadn't heard of it. The friend was aghast. "It happened three days ago!" she cried. Kingsolver responded that she was sorry for the Kennedy family, but this death did not affect her life any more than a death in her family would affect the Kennedys.

Bold, honest remarks such as this are interesting, stroking politely against the social grain.

One essay centers on a period of time when Kingsolver was editing an anthology of short stories and simultaneously dealing with multiple family crises. Admittedly a demanding reader, she tells how she decided which of 125 submitted stories would make the cut. A good story "will tell me something remarkable, it will be beautifully executed, and it will be nested in truth." That was her standard.

I applied that standard as I read through this volume and found most of the pieces, although non-fiction, come close to meeting it. One essay of carefully culled memories perfectly embodies her goals. It is titled "Letter to My Mother."

In a few brief pages, we meet Virginia Kingsolver as a young wife, wearing "happy red lipstick and red earrings," walking toward her daughter and swirling her skirt "like a rose with the perfect promise of you emerging from the center."

Years flow by, with struggles growing between independence and over-protectiveness. Misunderstandings rip the fabric of the mother-daughter bond. Little snapshots are dropped into the lap of the reader depicting Barbara in the arms of her mother or blanks when they are not speaking. Every word sounds genuine – a story beautifully executed and nested in remarkable truth.

A small wonder and, all by itself, worth the price of admission.

(*Small Wonder* by Barbara Kingsolver. HarperCollins, 2002. 264 pages)

Thank you, 'Jesus'
July 17, 2002

The most delicious reading experience for me is to open a favorite book for perhaps the 20th time and discover new delights and pleasures between old worn covers.

The second greatest experience is cracking the spine on a book by an author totally unknown and being captivated almost instantly by a new voice and a compelling story.

Last Year's Jesus by Ellen Slezak is a fabulous read of the second sort. A few paragraphs in and I knew I was hooked. That seldom happens with a collection of short stories, especially stories set in ... Detroit.

Detroit? You mean, where they make the cars? That Detroit?

Yet Detroit has its literary class. Elmore Leonard's crime novels qualify. Way back in the '70s, Arthur Hailey took a shot at the racy life of auto industry moguls, but he managed to bungle some important details. Also decades ago, Joyce Carol Oates, while teaching at a local university, cranked out some stories and a couple of novels – *Them* being the most familiar – using Detroit as a background. But her characters were less rooted in that particular city and might have existed in any decaying urban area.

Slezak's people are perfectly placed – they could live nowhere but Detroit.

She knows this territory cold: What the lawns and backyards look like, the beauty parlors, the pharmacies, the restaurants, grocery stores, boulevard and street names, cemeteries, churches and Tiger Stadium – you could draw a map from her descriptions.

I should know. Even though I haven't lived there for years, Detroit is my hometown.

This meticulous sense of place underpins Slezak's stories. The characters grow from a certain soil that is enriched with detail and smells right. She has planted her people with humor, sensitivity and unsparing honesty. You may not love all her characters, but you believe they are real and a few of them, 11-year-old Mona Palagolla is one, may break your heart.

The title story, "Last Year's Jesus (or Passion Play)," opens on a cold day with a young woman following the action through the Hamtramck (pronounced ham-TRAM-ick) section of the city, where clouds cover the participants "like a lid." A Mercy College student, orphaned and living with a strict Polish Catholic grandmother, the girl describes herself as six feet tall, plain, with an engine block of a body. "Everything about me – forehead, eyes, cheeks, shoulders, calves – is broad and uninterrupted by a mark of beauty or even an interesting defect." But she is not without fantasy.

As the procession marks the stations of the cross, horses draped in purple bathroom rugs and Mary clutching her blue pillowcase veil, our clumsy heroine is attracted to a gorgeous hunk who was Jesus in last year's play.

"Objectively speaking," she asks the reader, "as mortal beings, is there a road higher than sex with a man who'd been Jesus?"

The answer to that question involves a rival for the man who played Jesus, a nun and ultimate disappointment, but in the telling we are treated to a fascinating vignette.

In "Here in Car City," CeAnn buys the only building standing in a block of gritty burnouts – a small apartment house left vacant for nine months. Her mother shrieks, "In that neighborhood? Are you crazy? Even GM is moving out." But CeAnn creates Pensione Detroit because "car city needs some economical, cozy places to stay."

In "Patch," Sarah recalls how she and her lover Sam, noticing that businesses were closing around them and moving out, "decided to stay, to hold on to their little patch of Detroit for whatever it was worth."

Each of these stories highlights loyal Detroiters with no clear sense of their futures or even is which direction they should point themselves. They are like the city itself – hanging on and hoping for a better day. Tiny gains are made, but will they stick?

Although these characters don't seem to be going anywhere, I think the author definitely is. She has described a locality so well it seems to reflect the whole world. That's a literary gift.

Short stories tend to be neglected by the public until an author has produced a popular novel. I hear many discerning readers say they find stories unfulfilling. But this collection of nine stories and a brief novella is one to savor. Book groups should consider *Last Year's Jesus* for selection. I think they would find in these pages material provocative enough for riveting discussion.

Meanwhile, I will be first in line to buy a novel by Ellen Slezak whenever it appears, and I hope it's soon.

(*Last Year's Jesus* by Ellen Slezak. Hyperion Press, 2002. 237 pages)

On the 'Roads' again
July 26, 2002

Blame it on the heat index, which seems stuck at 110 degrees. Blame it on the fact that I'm not taking a vacation this summer, so a book title with the word "roads" in it seemed like a vicarious cheap thrill. Maybe it's the simple fact that I can't resist any scrap of information about those two deathless lovers Francesca Johnson and Robert Kincaid. Whatever the reason, I tagged along as Robert James Waller set off once again down *A Thousand Country Roads*.

This slim volume is not a sequel to Waller's mega-best-selling *The Bridges of Madison County*. He quite neatly wrapped that one up with the hero dying and never returning to requite his amorous adventure with a tenderly awakened farmwife. Rather, this novel is more of an in-fill. Waller imagines a brief interlude in Kincaid's life when he became involved with a young artist on the sands of Big Sur. The man's style seems to be affairs lasting only days.

That friendly coupling did not result in lifelong angst and pained desire, but it did produce a "boy-child," as Waller calls him. The son, Carlisle McMillan, now 36, has decided to search for his father.

The story begins in 1981, sixteen years after Robert Kincaid got lost driving down a dusty road, stopped at an Iowa farmhouse and met a woman who changed his life forever – and for 12 million readers worldwide, if you believe the publicity. Robert is 68, aching a bit in his bones but otherwise still a fine guy, chivalrous and highly principled, a poet-photographer-loner, the "last cowboy," though I've never figured out what he means by that description.

Kincaid has a hankering, a powerful yearning to connect with the most potent memory of his life. So he climbs into his old truck Harry – still running after 27 years of loyal service – with his trusty dog Highway and forty-three rolls of nearly extinct Tri-X black-and-white film, heads down the coast from Washington state and turns left for Iowa. At this exact moment, Carlisle begins his serious pursuit of the father who rode off on a motorcycle, never knowing what seeds were sown on a California beach.

Waller excels in careful plotting that brings characters oh-so-close. He is a minor genius at arranging his people in ways that display " ... the beauty of caprice." That's what Kincaid calls it when he glimpses objects coming together with an "elegance of whimsy" – belonging with each other in ways no human could manufacture.

So, while Kincaid is making his slow way back to Roseman Bridge and Francesca, sixty and still lovely, is performing her own ritual trudge to the site of her deepest happiness, Carlisle is on his way out to Seattle.

Two of these people never connect, which is so sad. You want them to be together, the same way you wanted Scarlett to win back Rhett.

It's not meant to be. Waller sets up too many roadblocks – reticent feelings, internal doubts, no forwarding addresses – the usual dead ends. But it leaves the reader feeling short-changed. Kincaid is passing through Mendocino, Calif., by utter chance meets that woman from Big Sur and recognizes her more than three decades after their romance. Yet he cannot make it back to Francesca, who has never budged from her kitchen during the sixteen years since they found the love of their lives.

Still, it's a heart-stopping scene where they're within sight of each other once again, only to miss because a snow storm blurs the vision. Sigh.

We have to make do with a tearful union of father and son in a Seattle jazz club. Kincaid entrusts Carlisle with carrying out his last request, to burn all the negatives and leave " ... the floor swept clean behind me, all traces gone, nothing left."

How I wish Waller would follow Kincaid's instructions. Unfortunately, he promises to carry on this saga someday in the story of Carlisle. I shall try to resist that temptation.

Novels like *Bridges* are publishing phenomena. Resembling bull markets, they move purely on momentum. One must read them because they're being read. The enduring popularity of this story was helped mightily by the film directed by Clint Eastwood. Memorable performances by Eastwood and, especially, Meryl

Streep, supported by the bluesy soundtrack and Richard LaGravenese's screenplay, took the material to a new level of thrilling drama and truth.

Here, however, Waller has not risen to new heights as a writer. He breaks no new ground. He's still doing his poor man's Hemingway larded over with new age-y poetry, accompanied by some distant music discernable to the author's ears alone.

Alas, that's not the point. People do experience love in strange and lasting moments, and we all try to make sense of the fragments of our lives. Sometimes, we succeed.

Considering everything, not a bad road trip.

(*A Thousand Country Roads: An Epilogue to The Bridges of Madison County* by Robert James Waller. John M. Hardy Publishing, 2002. 192 pages)

'Red Sky' is riveting
August 2, 2002

Eighteen-year-old Tami Oldham grabs her high school diploma and scampers off to Mexico in an old VW bus, clearly a girl seeking adventure.

By the time she is barely 23, this young woman has already experienced enough adventure for a lifetime, and so she has not been disappointed – and neither is the reader of her story.

Now, at age 42 and as Tami Oldham Ashcraft, with co-author Susea McGearhart, she has lived to tell a riveting tale in *Red Sky in Mourning: A True Story of Love, Loss, and Survival at Sea*.

Her odyssey begins as Tami is idling away her days on a surfing beach at Todos Santos and making a living selling her homegrown salsa to tourists. An ad on a restaurant bulletin board catches her attention. A cook is wanted on a boat leaving for

French Polynesia. She has to ask a friend what S/V means – "S-slash-V means sailing vessel, babe," is the answer.

A complete neophyte, Tami nevertheless gets the job and thus begins her life on the sea, a life of leaving possessions behind, making new friends in strange ports and warmly greeting old ones when paths cross. Tami opens her mind to fresh language and her heart to exotic climates while literally learning the ropes. Along the way, she also learns self-reliance and the craft of sailing.

Although this is a memoir and not a work of fiction, an impossibly romantic hero enters the scene. Richard Sharp is 11 years Tami's senior. Fascinating, rugged and British, he is circumnavigating the world in the cramped but audacious 36-foot *Mayaluga*, a boat he built himself from bow to stern. He invites Tami to sail with him to the South Pacific.

What follows are months of idyllic ocean cruising and stopping at lush islands while Richard and Tami are falling in love. Eventually, they are asked to deliver a yacht from Tahiti to San Diego, and Richard takes the job. With the money earned by this commission, he and Tami will be able to continue their adventure for another year at least.

On Sept. 22, 1983, Richard and Tami slip out of Papeete Harbor on the sleek and sexy 44-foot *Hazana*, bound for California. Recently engaged to be married, they radiate confidence and happiness, knowing that between the two of them, they have logged 50,000 miles at sea. They expect this voyage to take 30 days, after which they'll fly back to Tahiti and resume their course for New Zealand.

Twenty days out, the weather takes a bad turn. Very bad. A late-season storm, Hurricane Raymond, visits the yacht. Richard battles wind and rain courageously, tethering the two of them to the deck. Finally, he tells Tami to go below, which she does reluctantly. Almost immediately, she hears Richard scream, "OMIGOD!" and then she is knocked out.

When she awakes to silent chaos, Richard is gone. Later, she discovers she has been unconscious for 27 hours. She is injured, in shock, dizzy. Days pass before she can deal with her situation.

The boat has lost its mast and most of the sails. The disorder is such that she realizes *Hazana* not only had rolled over side to side, but also flipped end to end.

The story of how Tami rigs a small sail, sets a course, tends to her bruised body, grief, and despair and still manages to reach Hilo, Hawaii, tattered and tangled beyond belief after 41 days of solitary steering, is heart-stopping and inspiring.

When she discovers a fresh-water tank half full after Herculean efforts with hammer and chisel, the reader wants to shout and dance along with Tami. "I did every dance I had ever learned: the watusi, the jerk, the swim – winding down with a sexy bump and grind." You go, girl!

Stories of perilous sea voyages – men in open boats grappling with storms, starvation and thirst – grip the soul. Ernest Shackleton, Thor Heyerdahl, Capt. Bligh – the very names evoke thrilling memories of reading about their harrowing adventures in snug and safe quarters.

In many ways, Tami Oldham's saga surpasses these more famous yarns. Utterly alone except for an inner "Voice" that kept her sane, young yet wise, afraid yet intrepid, she survived because of solid skills and her ability to use a sextant.

Some of the most interesting parts of the story involve what happened after the disaster. To this day, Tami Oldham Ashcraft sails and encourages those who dream of a life on the sea, which she calls "the complete life – full of adventure, education, freedom and fun." Her only caution is not to tempt Mother Nature by sailing during any portion of hurricane season.

It was gratifying to read that this spirited and intelligent woman, a decade after her ordeal, married a talented and good man, and thus reached safe harbor – twice.

(*Red Sky in Mourning: A True Story of Love, Loss, and Survival at Sea* by Tami Oldham Ashcraft and Susea McGearhart. Hyperion, 2002. 223 pages)

A sweet slice of 'Pie'
August 8, 2002

"I am worth a story. Everybody is. Ask Rose," declares Ruth Pirkle.

I'd like to do just that. Except the opening line in Catherine Landis's inviting first novel, *Some Days There's Pie*, tells us, "Rose is dead." The year is 1979 and Rose is as old as the century.

The story of this remarkable character is told to us by Ruth, a young woman growing up in near poverty in a family she doesn't understand in Summerville, Tenn. – a place no one's ever heard of. Ruth lives next to Lonnie's Kwik Pik, an Esso station, and Durwood's Hardware where, at 18, she sells fried pies baked by Durwood's wife, Mabel Jones.

The pies are so popular, they alone draw customers to the store. But some days, Mabel just doesn't feel like making pies, and Ruth reports that those were "the sad days. People left with their heads hanging low, and I was the one who had to break it to them. But it's like everything else; some days there's pie, some days there's not."

I would add that this book is like the aisles in Durwood's store: on some pages there's pie, and on others nuts and bolts.

The novel takes us into Southern territory where people eat heavy food and don't worry about it, where families and friends all get into one another's business, and where scents like fried chicken and peach pie blend wonderfully with cow manure.

Ruth's aimless life is given a sudden jolt when she runs off and marries Chuck Pirkle, a flashy stereo salesman who is leaving Summerville and "leaving Summerville was the exact thing I had wanted to do all my life."

Ruth insists she never plans anything ahead of time – she didn't even know she was going away until she stepped into Chuck's car. So it's plausible when she abruptly leaves him some months later after he turns into a religious fanatic.

This time, she steps into her own car, a beat-up 1971 Datsun 210, and takes off for – anywhere. Ruth lands in Lawsonville, N.C., and, fainting from hunger and fatigue, she literally is scraped off the floor by Rose Lee. In that moment of connection, the stories of these two women intertwine.

Rose is the wise, nurturing female and source of unconditional love that Ruth has been seeking. Ruth does not see Rose as old or past her time. Each becomes protective of the other, and Ruth does need help. She only thinks she can handle herself around men, and she possesses no professional skills. She never seems to eat a regular meal yet tosses back a fair number of cold beers every day. In fact, almost everyone in town seems to drink as casually as they gossip.

For decades, Rose and her husband Raymond owned and ran the Chocowin County Crier, a small but intrepid weekly newspaper. Rose became famous for her investigative reporting, breaking stories of corruption and keeping the locals honest. She also wrote personal profiles of anyone she considered interesting and that included everyone in the county.

It all ended when Raymond was killed by a train. When Ruth meets her, Rose is managing to hold onto a job with the Lawsonville Ledger – in advertising. Not a writing job and not influential, but she craves working even though she has lung cancer and heart trouble.

It seems everyone wants Rose to slow down and, for her own good of course, simply quit. Yet Ruth encourages her to sniff out a story of graft in the county's health department. Rose gets the goods, including incriminating photos, but she is prevented from publishing her story by a too-timid editor.

Landis works with a large cast of characters and tries to cover a lot of ground. Some careful pruning might have been in order to tighten the pace and narrative flow, but the book is rich in humor and authentic details of small town newspaper ambience, a reflection of the author's own experiences.

How Ruth manages to spirit Rose away from her well-meaning daughters' clutches to take her on one last trip home, and how in attempting that feat, Ruth finally is able to go home herself make a touching and poignant finale.

I do not mean to aggrandize this pleasant novel beyond its level of competence, but there is something noble and catching in Rose's final struggle to get on the road again, in Ruth feeding her M&Ms and Coke in a crazy cabin in the mountains. It made me think – don't laugh – of Tolstoy's spare death in a railway station a few miles from his estate, of what valor exists in a sick and dying individual who refuses to lie down.

There are many stories of improbable relationships that change lives forever. This one lingers in the heart for a while. Rose is dead, but Rose is very much alive.

I hope Catherine Landis owns the ingredients for mixing up another pie.

(*Some Days There's Pie* by Catherine Landis. St. Martin's Press, 2002. 291 pages)

Please open 'The God File'
August 16, 2002

My first reaction after reading *The God File* by Frank Turner Hollon was, "This is a great book." Several days later, my opinion has not changed.

The God File would be a good read if only for the clear, arresting voice of the narrator, Gabriel Black, and compelling because of the page-turning suspense of the man's uncertain fate.

It is far easier to talk about why a novel is good than make the case for greatness – an elusive quality usually decided between the author and each individual reader – the difference between craft and art.

I call it great because I felt as though Hollon were sitting beside me and breathing his story into my ear alone. The book is done so well, is so lacking in contrivance as to seem effortless. The author has what I call "leadership" – the ability to grab you and take you somewhere and you don't want to let go of his hand.

In this case it's especially true because the action takes place in a dismal maximum-security prison.

The premise is deceptively simple: In his mid-20s, for reasons unfathomable even to him, Gabriel Black confessed to a capital murder he did not commit and has remained incarcerated for 22 years. During that time, he became an avid reader, collecting snippets of stories, memories and observations giving evidence that God exists. These constitute the "God file" – slight passages of one or two pages, each one a chapter in the book, a few dozen in all.

If T. S. Eliot showed us fear in a handful of dust, Hollon shows us faith and a quest for the meaning of life in a motley bundle of scribbles kept in a cardboard box and shoved under a bunk in a prison cell.

Gabriel Black turns the expression "The Devil is in the details" on its head to interpret God in the details. As his fellow inmate John tells it, "We simply do not have the time, or take the time, to explore the little details. But when a person is in prison, ... all he has are the little details to explore."

Gabriel explores all the "disgusting sadness" of his life and almost in the same sentence declares that the next moment is a gift. There are passages in this book so luminous and precise – on simple silence or the smell of a baseball glove and, so true, about orgasm resembling poison ivy – that you simply don't know whether to cry or shout for joy. If you are also a writer, you might want to pack up and go home.

Of course, it had to be about a woman – the enigmatic and unworthy Janie Fitzpatrick. Janie was ... is ... the love of Gabriel's life. It was for her that he took the rap of life imprisonment with no parole and she has never thanked nor once visited him.

In the brown box are several letters Gabriel has written to Janie. These letters form a brilliant progression of his state of mind as he moves from hopefulness to despair to acceptance. They serve as terse pleadings that become expressive prayers and might have been written to God Himself.

Janie does not respond. She is a vanished presence.

One summer long ago in Paris, Ernest Hemingway sat down to write four true sentences. Frank Hollon has beaten that record by the hundreds. He writes about fire and football, families and depravity and killing and the weather, and it seems as though you are reading about these ordinary things for the first time.

It would demean this book to mention a "faith journey" or redemption or blather on about a soul struggling with his dark side. This book is not even about religion. It is philosophy of a lofty order discovered through gritty reality.

Gabriel is the highest ranking archangel of the Hebrew, Christian and Muslim religions. By the end of this unusual and expert novel, his namesake is soaring, lifting us also.

I hope Frank Hollon finds the audience he deserves. Perhaps it will begin in a college classroom. A daring professor might decide to scrap the musty text of Descartes and his endless proofs of the existence of a Supreme Being and assign *The God File* instead.

What an exalted act that would be!

(*The God File* by Frank Turner Hollon. MacAdam/Cage, 2002. 147 pages)

'Metal' is pure grade
August 23, 2002

I was reluctant to pick up and begin reading *The Metal Shredders* by Nancy Zafris, but I did and then I could not put it down.

Why the initial hesitation? It's about scrap metal – isn't that reason enough?

I'm glad I overcame my petty objection, because otherwise I would have missed a funny, intriguing and smartly written novel by a writer I'm delighted to know.

The proper subject matter for literature is an old debated topic. Hemingway declared war to be the "great subject," and nothing else came close. Jane Austen slyly murmured she wrote only about love and money. But truthfully, there is no subject that, with a fair amount of wit and skill and a little genius, cannot be shaped into art. This book is a good example. It's about money and family and the scrap business.

Calvin Coolidge said the business of America is business. John Bonner & Son Metal Shredders spans three generations of a family-owned and operated business in Ohio. What could be more American?

As this novel begins, the grandfather – the patriarch and original shredder who started by scavenging scrap along the roadside – has died. His old friends and competitors stand around the coffin, testing it for "pull" using magnets attached to their key chains. They all pronounce the casket a disgrace. It is yellow brass, not copper as the old man wanted.

Their conversations, their blood, their lives translate into a hierarchy of metal – pure grade, alloy, contaminants. Who would have guessed that the scrap business is as caste-driven as New Delhi or Victorian England?

The company is left in the hands of the "Senior" Bonner but is really run by the grandson, John, a handsome guy of 30 who cannot get over being abandoned by his wife, Elise. A daughter, Octavia, or Otty, a Wellesley graduate now 34, has returned home from a wandering sojourn in Spain and a loveless affair in Boston. She is pretending to learn the business.

Clashes between the Senior and son naturally erupt. John is "the same exact height as the Senior only a lot shorter." You get the picture. The Senior exerts an iron will over the scrap yard and the employees – even in his increasing absences from the office.

For instance, he insists, just because he can, that John and Tony, a young shredder wannabe, clean up a Ford LTD dumped there by the police. The car had housed two dead and decaying bodies for weeks and emits a permanent stench. But because the car has only 51,000 miles on it, the Senior wants it beautified so he can sell it for a greater profit than it would bring as scrap.

It turns out the trunk is full of money – highly odorous money – and John and Tony go through contortions to clean and hide and deal with this stash.

The characters are certainly interesting, the narrative and subplots are provocative and the dead-on humor slaps you silly.

"He's getting that mortally wounded turtle look," John muses about a co-worker. Yet the fascination of this book is definitely the business itself, carefully and even lovingly detailed. The huge shredder dominates the yard. Forbidding heavy equipment, all manner of gear and stuff denote a dangerous and complicated place. So much is told about crunching and smashing and screeching that one listens to this novel as much as reads it.

Is it too much information? I don't think so. The particulars become a kind of music, another way of expressing emotion, much like the paragraphs without end about weaponry hardware in a Tom Clancy novel. You don't have to get it all to get it.

One firm rule of drama is that if a gun is introduced in Act I, it must be fired in Act III. We learn early on about an employee who was accidentally shredded back during the grandfather's day. As the giant machine eats its way through flattened automobiles, broken fences and whole buildings, and as the power plays become more defined among the characters, you know a human sacrifice is necessary. Nancy Zafris does not disappoint.

Many books are written about businesses – the fashion industry, Hollywood, politics, executive suite intrigue – but the work part frequently seems fake, just an excuse to write about the ways people beat up on each other. Here, Zafris has done her homework. The book is, above all, real.

The Metal Shredders nails it.

(*The Metal Shredders* by Nancy Zafris (Blue Hen Books/Penguin Putnam, 2002. 291 pages)

The 'Greatest' Lincoln
August 29, 2002

In the aftermath of September 11, 2001, a call-in program on the public affairs network C-SPAN asked listeners to share what works they were reading for comfort and inspiration in these turbulent times. A large measure of the audience reported turning to works about Abraham Lincoln and the Civil War.

A worthy offering in that category is the compact and thrilling dissection of *Lincoln's Greatest Speech: The Second Inaugural* by Ronald C. White, Jr.

With admirable economy, White gives us Lincoln the man, the politician, the orator and (my interpretation) the saint at his most thoughtful and brilliant moment, 41 days before his assassination.

The book is simple in form. White sets the scene in the first chapter and then devotes each succeeding chapter to one paragraph of the address – a mere 703 words in all, delivered in seven minutes of Lincoln's slow, deliberate speech. Included, and of great value, are a facsimile of the speech in Lincoln's handwriting and a prescient photograph, the only one of Lincoln speaking, which shows John Wilkes Booth among the spectators.

The day was March 4, 1865. Rain and wind had turned the nation's capital into a sea of mud. Still, more than 50,000 people streamed into town. Eyewitnesses testify to their "good-natured" tolerance of the conditions. Almost half the crowd was African-American, dressed in bright colors and best finery.

A phenomenon recorded in several accounts describes the moment when Lincoln began to speak. The rain ceased, the clouds blew away and a peaceful and lovely sunshine poured down from the sky.

Yet Lincoln faced an audience anxious in mood. The war was not quite over; Lee's surrender at Appomattox remained a month away. The nation had endured unthinkable carnage and ruin both in property and the loss of 620,000 lives and was still deeply divided on what appeared to be an uncertain peace. Lincoln's task – to calm, instruct and heal – was mighty.

Resolutely, he spoke the immortal words that Frederick Douglass, present at the speech, later told the president were "more like a sermon than a state paper."

In our present day of speech writers and ghost writers, it is wonderful to contemplate this great leader, taking a pencil stub and scribbling on cardboard boxes, his favorite writing material, to create the address that is today carved in marble on his memorial.

White acknowledges the phrase "With malice toward none; with charity for all..." as the most quoted of the speech. He calls them "sacred words" and "Lincoln's legacy to the nation." As he explicates each paragraph and phrase, referring to Lincoln's thoughts and ideas as they evolved during his life, White re-creates the moment of the speech in a way that is whole and alive.

As a professor of theology, White is particularly adept at analyzing Lincoln's biblical references and putting them in context. His discussion of the meaning of the word "charity" is especially insightful.

Notwithstanding White's credentials as a scholar, the appeal of this book lies in his affectionate and admiring descriptions of Lincoln as a young man and later statesman, struggling to "overcome his own physical appearance to win the right to be heard."

White devotes a satisfying portion of his text to helping the reader understand how Lincoln sounded when he spoke, and how he labored over his speeches, punctuating them for the ear.

Fascination with Abraham Lincoln began in his day and has remained high. His personality is too large to be contained in any one volume. It is gratifying that White has come up with fresh interpretations and commentary. The book is crammed with illuminating details. The story of the Fort Pillow massacre that prompted the commander's widow, Mary Booth, to ask for pensions for the common-law wives of slain black soldiers – and Lincoln's getting this legislation passed – offers reason enough to read this account.

It is often said Abraham Lincoln could not be elected president today because he would not do well on television. After reading the history of this one speech, I'm convinced this is utterly untrue; Lincoln would be a compelling presence on TV. Even as a young man, thirsting with ambition, Lincoln knew he had to present himself in the public arena to win people's attention and confidence. Fully aware of his awkward manners and looks, he used his wit and personal magnetism to become the man Pablo Picasso called "the greatest American."

Although Picasso amassed a huge collection of Lincoln memorabilia, he never attempted a portrait. That seems appropriate. It is clear from White's book that Lincoln's true portrait is in his words, written and spoken.

"Neither vindication nor triumphalism is present in the Second Inaugural. At the bedrock is Lincoln's humility," declares White. The man agonized over how to go forward with justice and reconciliation, not falling into an easy "God Bless America" theology but confronting our own ambiguities and hypocrisies.

Lincoln presents few answers and instead encourages us to ask difficult questions – exactly what we need, always but especially now, as White so beautifully reminds us.

(*Lincoln's Greatest Speech: The Second Inaugural* by Ronald C. White, Jr. Simon & Schuster, 2002. 203 pages)

Deep thoughts of 'Command'
September 6, 2002

The subject of war is everywhere these days, impossible to avoid. Newscasts and talk shows devote hours to discussion and debate as to whether the United States should invade Iraq, with or without the sanction of "the world community."

Polls are conducted hourly to discern the wishes of the country and some days it seems no action will be taken until the considered opinion of each citizen is recorded and thrown into the decision-making process.

At times like these, it is soothing to dip into history, partly as a way of organizing one's thoughts and attempting to see our present options in some sort of context.

So I turned to John Keegan, our finest living military historian. Any one of his books, all of which thankfully remain in print, yields rich rewards, but I chose his original and perceptive classic work *The Mask of Command*. In our modern era of smart bombs and precision-guided missiles and the mutually assured destructive capability of nuclear weapons, it is somehow consoling to read of black powder wars, hand-to-hand combat and heroic leadership.

What this leadership consists of, its makeup and execution, Keegan describes through reviewing the careers of four men: Alexander the Great, the Duke of Wellington, Ulysses S. Grant and – amazingly but justly – Adolph Hitler. Taking each in turn, as he discusses the various personal histories, character traits and major battle techniques, Keegan treats us to sharp insights on the development of weaponry, methods of assault, the social context of armies within their societies, and all sorts of lively and illuminating details of warfare.

"He had the historian's ability to summarize events and incorporate them smoothly in the larger narrative," Keegan writes of Grant's memoirs, but he could easily be describing his own talents. It is impossible to imagine any better telling of these stories, or more thrilling narrative, that gives both the grand and, in his word, "grisly" nature of what this history is all about.

Although he includes a solid bibliography, Keegan dispenses with distracting footnotes. Along with troop positions on sweeping battlefields, he gives us the small moments of a soldier struggling with, "that dribble of unmanning fear" as he faces the enemy.

If a book about men who lead others to death can be enthralling, this is it.

Keegan poses the central and important question at the heart of any commander's examination of conscience: Where must I place myself? Always in front, sometimes, never? Keegan proceeds to examine each commander's style, thought process and behavior in light of this question.

Alexander was always in front, in full conspicuous battle gear, driving his men forward, depending on the example of his physical courage and spiritual strength as their king.

This was a man who began every day by plunging his sword into a living animal as a blood sacrifice to the gods. He spent most of his brief but epic life either on the battlefield or preparing for battle. By all accounts, he enjoyed convivial feasts that sometimes turned into sloshing brawls, but he kept himself highly informed in matters of topography and culture wherever he sought to conquer.

Alexander's army triumphed through sheer muscle strength. Keegan's description of its signature offensive weapon, the human phalanx, is stirring. Imagine a unit of powerful men each carrying an 18-foot iron-tipped spear, packed together in eight ranks and moving as one giant beast, "unapproachable by either infantry or cavalry as long as they kept their nerve and cohesion."

Nerve and cohesion appear to be the keys to success as Keegan traverses 2,000 years of command.

Wellington, the Iron Duke, and Grant shared qualities with Alexander. All enjoyed good health and possessed the wonderful attribute of being able to sleep well even during times of enormous stress and responsibility. Keegan emphasizes how clean and particular were their habits. Wellington and Grant both preferred a simple diet, although the Duke's meals were prepared and served by his huge entourage of cooks and servants. Grant never had a servant.

These men exuded intrepid coolness in the face of danger and issued concise, even elegant orders in the thick of combat. While Wellington and Grant sometimes got into the fray, they did not purposely place themselves at the head of columns of soldiers. They dressed plainly and worked the scene of battle from vantage points where they could most clearly ascertain what orders were most effective to achieve victory.

Hitler, on the other hand, never placed himself close to his men or any of the fronts over which he made himself supreme commander.

Keegan's treatment of Hitler among these field generals is fascinating. He respectfully recounts Hitler's record in World War I and credits him with truly earning the right to call himself first soldier of the Reich.

Keegan then goes on to detail the insomniac Hitler's style of command as remote, petulant, "pettifogging" on minute particulars, uninformed about the larger picture, rambling and indecisive when giving orders, surrounding himself with sycophants.

Keegan names this style "false heroic." His inclusion of this wretched and ultimately insane commander in a work on heroic leadership gives balance and breadth to a profession that otherwise would seem overly admirable and even romantic.

In his conclusion, perhaps the least successful section because it seems truncated, Keegan considers the future of command in the nuclear age. We are far from the days of a general's autonomy, when Grant could say, "I did not communicate my plan to the President."

Keegan makes the case that generals should not own the critical decisions of using force; rather that these burdens should lie solely with presidents and prime ministers. Although the most lauded military leaders of the past have been men unafraid to act and act decisively, Keegan believes what might be needed is a leader of modesty, prudence and rationality who chooses, "not to act, in any traditionally heroic sense, at all."

Amid all the chatter it is worth considering what Keegan, who knows almost everything about this subject, thinks about both the history and future of heroic leadership.

(*The Mask of Command* by John Keegan. Viking Adult, 1987. 368 pages)

A real 'Nowhere Man'
September 13, 2002

When I turned the final page of Aleksandar Hemon's powerfully written novel, *Nowhere Man*, I wanted to talk and talk about it until someone would tell me – politely or not – to just calm down and shut up.

I found details so closely observed and implications for life and memory so large that reading this story reminded me of watching the film "Dr. Zhivago."

On the page are Hemon's equivalents of David Lean's caressing camera lingering over images such as Lara's wilting sunflowers, a bare tree branch tickling a cold window pane or Yuri's pen dipping into thawed ink, while something huge and terrifying lurks constantly in the background, shaping the characters' lives and decisions, threatening at any moment to jerk the story in some new direction.

Hemon himself has been driven in multiple directions. A native of Yugoslavia and student of world literature, he published several stories before traveling to the United States in 1992 at the age of 28. When war broke out in Sarajevo, he became stranded here and, deciding to continue his literary career, gave himself five years to learn and publish in English.

Lucky for us, he is some kind of linguistic genius, and his stories began appearing in 1995. His first novel, *The Question of Bruno*, excited literary critics everywhere and introduced the interesting character Jozef Pronek who becomes the Nowhere Man in the current title.

An unnamed narrator begins the story in an ESL classroom in Chicago in 1994 then switches back to Yugoslavia and Pronek's childhood, where we see young Jozef playfully torturing a mouse.

Mice remain a recurring theme in the novel, which is also dense with imagery of pairing and coupling: Siamese twins, roommates with similar lineage and a series of sweetly recalled "first loves." An endearing example is the rock band of two, called Bube (Serbo-Croatian for beetle) that Pronek dreams up with his boyhood friend Mirza. The idea for the band springs from the joy of these adolescents discovering rock and roll and deviously acquiring a Beatles songbook.

Crooning "Yeah, Yeah, Yeah" and "He's a real nowhere man, sitting in his nowhere land," they charm girls and wow their friends. In their mid-teens, they add two members, and the name segues into Blind Jozef Pronek and Dead Souls, performing dreadful blues music composed by Pronek. It is all so young and hopeful. The songs express that "feeling of pleasant soul pain, when you are at peace with your woeful life."

As the narrator recalls, "Sarajevo in the eighties was a beautiful place to be young – I know because I was young then. I remember linden trees blooming as if they were never to bloom again, producing the smell that I can feel in my nostrils now. The boys were handsome, the girls beautiful, the sports teams successful, the bands good, the streets felt as soft as a Persian carpet, and the Winter Olympics made everyone feel that we were at the center of the world."

After an extended affair with the bewitching Sabina, whom Pronek first ogles at a nightclub, followed by a stint in the army, we see him in full manhood during a summer in Kiev in the Ukraine through the enamored eyes of fellow student Victor Plavchuk. Victor prizes Jozef's "ability to respond and speak to the world" – the very traits that also draw in the reader.

As things are turning ugly in Croatia, Pronek's life begins a zigzagging course. In a line parallel to the author's own biography, he lands in Chicago to commence plodding efforts of assimilation into this vastly different culture. His world splinters as he tries to keep informed of the terrible killing and devastation at home, taking various low-paying, thankless jobs and working on his English while a slow disintegration of identity occurs.

The narrator, an increasingly defined presence, keeps us informed of (the now) Joseph's weird dreams, of his disorientation, at times extreme. He loses a sense of reality, constantly closing his eyes and hoping he will open them in a different place.

Bumbling Americans just don't get him or the war as it unfolds on television.

"What are you?" asks one crude employer. "It's Serbs fighting Muslims over there, right? Are you Serb or Muslim?"

"I am complicated," answers Pronek. "You can say I am the Bosnian."

He grapples with the reality of the war while many around him think it's somehow all faked. Lovely Sabina meets a terrible fate, and his own mother is almost killed when a bomb falls on a market in Sarajevo. He has forgotten all the music.

In a shattering climax, Pronek demolishes a tiny rodent in a middle-of-the-night rage. This act yields a tour de force passage brilliantly defining total breakdown – a panorama of the humor and crazy sense and nonsense of life – where fear and force do battle for survival against a furry little mouse.

Although *Nowhere Man* reads easily, this novel is not easy and requires a certain commitment on the part of the reader. The narration does not move in linear fashion, and you must truly pay attention. If you love good writing, I guarantee you'll be kept going by dazzling literary pyrotechnics that explode on almost every page.

My own mousy fear is that I won't do this novel justice in a brief review. So I beg earnest book groups to give this author his due. You'll earn a rich reward.

(*Nowhere Man* by Aleksandar Hemon. Doubleday, 2002. 232 pages)

Women scorned writing 'Letters'
September 20, 2002

"He was her man, but he done her wrong."

The old lyric about Frankie and Johnny is fitting accompaniment to *Hell Hath No Fury: Women's Letters from the End of the Affair*, edited by Anna Holmes. In the endless drama between men and women, here we have numerous renderings of the final act.

Let me state upfront: Men, you will not like this book. You might even want to quit reading this review. This particular Hell cries out for pouring wine, grabbing hankies and calling a girlfriend.

The book, Holmes tells us, was "borne out of anger, humiliation, disbelief and disgust." Two months into a relationship, she was dumped by an emotionally immature guy she calls Arthur. Turning to a familiar outlet for pain, she tapped out a scathing e-mail, hit SEND then copied it to her 10 best friends. Their sympathetic and supportive responses spurred Holmes to collect these letters, ranging from highly literate to stormy to weepy and pathetic.

Quite honestly, I expected giddy fun and even vicarious guilty pleasure. Letters provide the perfect forum to say just what you wish you could think of in a moment of white heat. I was hoping for nothing less than outright justice for women scorned.

But that was not the case. Love and life are too complex.

The letters – more than 100, both real and fictional – span over 2,000 years. Some are lengthy and poetic, but most are brief. Holmes prefaces each one so the reader understands the circumstances under which it was written.

As in the recent film "Possession," the volume illuminates how we are affected, even after centuries have passed, by the immediacy and intimacy of letters. Unfortunately, here – unlike in that film – we are given only one side of romance, and dying romance at that. The men who are the objects of all this emotion just kind of slink away. The constant themes weaving through the missives disparage men's elusiveness and lack of commitment, robbing women of their best years – or months – and the fact that, for whatever reasons, they just cease to care.

I think I detect an answer to Freud's famous question: What does woman want? Dear God, what does she want?

If Holmes's anthology is at all accurate, she wants the man to stand there and somehow take it. The letters plead: Hear me! But countless of them read like feeble parting shots lamely fired at an enemy disappearing over the hill.

Fascinating, though a little voyeuristic, to scan letters by Sylvia Plath, Anne Sexton and Edith Wharton. It is heartrending to think of how often women are well and truly abandoned. It is also possible to conclude these women simply chose badly.

What are we to make of a series of letters (unsent, by the way) that a writer and filmmaker wrote to each of a dozen boyfriends over a period of 10 years, enumerating all their faults and terrible habits and general unworthiness? I mean, duh, who was picking these guys?

One ends up learning a lot more about the women themselves than the men they so love/hate/care about and despise/never-want-to-see-again/please come over. The title promises energizing anger, a cleansing response. In so many, it is apparent the women blame themselves and are caustic rather than effective.

The book is handily organized into sections such as "The Tell-Off," "The Divorce Letter," "The Classic" and so on. The most crushing chapter is the one titled "Dear John." It's sad picturing these utterly blameless men opening notes saying, in effect, "I hope you can forgive me, but..."

Holmes includes ample references for her research along with the lengthiest list of acknowledgments I have ever seen. Yet the book seems hastily thrown together. There are so many print errors that it becomes distracting after a while. I think these earnest letters deserved better. It has only been since the fall of 2000 that Holmes gave Arthur (definitely not a knight in shining armor) the brush-off that started all this. Why the rush?

Now, my own parting shot: On the ugly and off-putting cover, a harsh-looking woman with coarse blond hair shrieks through angry red lips. It looks so loud you want to cover your ears.

For this volume of letters written in private sorrow and/or wrath, wouldn't it have been better to show a woman dabbing at her eyes while furiously scribbling? Or, perhaps, staring at a computer screen while we glimpse dawn breaking through the window over her shoulder?

Just a thought.

(*Hell Hath No Fury: Women's Letters from the End of the Affair*, edited by Anna Holmes. Carroll & Graf, 2002. 432 pages)

Dining on 'Lobster'
September 27, 2002

In an English literature class some decades ago, we were asked to summarize *Moby Dick* in one sentence. The best response was judged to be: A man goes fishing.

Using that exercise with Linda Greenlaw's *The Lobster Chronicles: Life on a Very Small Island,* I would offer: A woman goes fishing but doesn't make a catch.

Greenlaw first appeared on the literary scene a few years back as a minor character in Sebastian Junger's wildly popular tale *A Perfect Storm*. She was captain of the 100-foot swordfish boat

Hannah Boden. After 17 years in that career – a singular one for a woman – she returned home to live on Isle au Haut (pronounced I-la-HOE), a tiny island 7 miles off the coast of Maine, and took up lobster fishing in her 35-foot *Mattie Belle*.

It turns out that the business of fishing for lobsters is not as picturesque and romantic as it seems when one is breezing through quaint coastal villages and seeing the cheerful painted buoys bobbing on the waves. Those buoys, hundreds of them, must be hauled, scraped, painted and stored – and that is one of the more pleasant jobs. Greenlaw is good at describing the sheer volume of physical labor it takes to do her work. It's impressive – also dirty and stinking and endless.

She tells a dual story here. The first recounts one season of trapping lobsters, and the second tells the history and present situation of her beloved island. The Island, as Greenlaw refers to it, is where she grew up. She writes with affection, humor and frustration of what it's like to live among a population of 70 people and be related to almost half of them. The Island's individuals are hardy, but the community is fragile. Most of the young eventually move away, understandably so, considering the limited employment opportunities and the difficult, lonely winters.

The Islanders, though welcoming some summer visitors, choose not to beef up a tourist industry but rather rely on the renewable resource of lobsters. In most years, the crustaceans provide a booming business. In the year of this story, however, the lobsters are not appearing, and people are worried. Islanders meet to discuss the over-fishing by outsiders in Isle au Haut's territorial waters. There's talk of war over the encroachment. Yet something also seems wrong with the lobsters. Greenlaw and her father, retired and working with her as sternman, spend many days hauling up empty traps only to re-bait and send them back into the deep. They call this depressing effort "changing the water."

Greenlaw begins to question her life choices in a real way. Part of the charm of this book is her absolutely candid confession that one of the reasons she left her life on the sea was her desire to find a man and begin a family. She jokes about her life being a metaphor of fishing and trapping with matrimony in mind. As it hasn't happened so far, she muses about the possible reasons, saying, "I wondered if other people spent as much time as I do wondering."

Time for wondering is a plentiful commodity for one who spends a great deal of it alone. "Talking is not one of my needs," she writes. Perhaps that person is perfectly suited for island living. But I wonder why a woman who wants to get married would choose to live in a place where there are no eligible men. None. Still, Greenlaw is cheerily unabashed in declaring, more than once, that she is looking for Mr. Right, even though he "does not appear to be looking for me."

In one of those quirks of reading, I began to think of Calamity Jane, living in a man's world out on the Dakota frontier, self-reliant and using salty language, surrounded by men yet unmarried. A few pages later, the author herself references Jane. It occurred to me that it's difficult to be both one of the boys and taken seriously as a woman.

In the meantime, Greenlaw amuses herself becoming reacquainted with all the interesting and colorful characters who inhabit the Island. There is Ted Hoskins, minister of the Congregational church, who looks like God – if He wore glasses – and Victor Richards, an ex-crop-dusting pilot who eats cigars and brings "the Alabama Slammer" over from the mainland, surely the flashiest (in the obvious sense) gal the Islanders have seen in a century. A reader could end up comparing life on the Island to that of a coed fraternity, a somewhat closed society whose members alternate between niggling over issues of interest only to themselves and bawdy fun.

Greenlaw writes poetically of water and bracing wind and the mating of lobsters. She reserves some of her finest passages for loving portraits of her parents and the Island spirit they embody. The scene of her mother smashing dishes when told that her daughter would be taking her degree from Colby College and going off to work on a swordfish boat is indelible. Almost as good is the vignette of her dad patiently explaining to mainlanders why they weren't catching any lobsters in the trees.

It is not a contradiction to say that Greenlaw is a great storyteller but not always a good writer. She indulges in too many unoriginal musings about what she thinks of dogs or how it feels to wake up in the morning. Yet when she sticks to her strengths, this is a brisk and engaging read. Much drama is provided by the sorrow of empty traps and the diagnosis of her mother's cancer.

Greenlaw's consistently and refreshingly honest view of her life has one rooting for her. At the end of the book, the permanent population of the Island has shrunk to 47, but she is building a house and thinking about perhaps going out to sea again.

While reading the history and lore of these Islanders, I occasionally wanted to shake them out of their inbred lives and isolation, and toss them into the world to earn decent money. But then they would be just like everyone else. I ended up grateful for this genuine memoir and hoping these people will be able to preserve their eccentric but appealing way of life.

For who among us does not dream of islands?

(*The Lobster Chronicles: Life on a Very Small Island* by Linda Greenlaw. Hyperion, 2002. 235 pages)

Mixed 'Blessings'
October 4, 2002

The success of an Anna Quindlen novel is assured. Critics roll out the drums and trumpets and customers line up in bookstores hugging multiple copies. This is a writer who connects with a wide and loyal audience.

So I began to read *Blessings*, her latest, with some hope. Perhaps this one would finally do it for me. But alas, I found it as unsatisfying and overpraised as her earlier efforts.

Blessings is the beautiful ancestral home of Lydia Blessing, an 80-year-old widow who has retreated into cloistered existence at this shrine to her past. Located near a town called Mount Mason, somewhere I think in Pennsylvania, the setting is portrayed as a timeless place where little ever changes. Wealthy and imperious, Lydia controls every aspect of her domain, from the hour coffee shall brew to the proper pinching of her bachelor buttons.

It naturally follows that such a woman would hire a hapless kid she meets in a Walmart parking lot when her battery needs a jump. Skip Cuddy moves into the garage apartment at Blessings and proceeds to make her morning coffee and manage the vast property like a champ, even though his previous jobs have been in fast food and the mall cineplex and the laundry room at the county jail. He has just finished serving 10 months for driving the getaway car during a Quik-Stop robbery. He's basically a good guy who made a poor choice of friends.

So, after a month on the new job, when a day-old baby girl is left on the driveway by his doorstep, he instantly claims her and secretly takes care of her, strapping her to his chest as he drives the lawnmower or whatever. He runs around buying formula and equipment from yard sales – just what you'd expect from a 20-year-old who'd been practically orphaned and brought up in various homes of relatives or a friend's trailer, who'd spent most of his "adult" life hanging out in bars with wrong types. Sure.

Eventually, Lydia gets into the act along with Jennifer, the exemplary daughter of her housekeeper. They idle away the summer, watching the baby grow and thrive. Passage after passage describes adorable little Faith, her smiles and the way she looks at trees and grabs your finger – all the cute baby stuff. Meanwhile, Skip rejuvenates the estate.

Suddenly, he seems to know all about pruning orchards and repairing antique barns. Lydia muses and ponders and mucks around in her long but mostly uninteresting past, endlessly recalling her childhood when "the days were so long and the years somehow so short."

Even with the large type and plenty of white space, these 200 or so pages seem like a long, slow read – that somehow comes up short. Reading this book is similar to being forced into viewing someone's faded album, listening to the droning narrative about people you don't know, trying to stay focused while your mind wanders.

Quindlen coyly doles out information, revealing tidbits almost stingily, such as the big secret about Lydia's brother, Sunny. The problem is, the reader has figured it out on page 24. The action of the book covers three months – but it seems to take a lot longer to get to everyone's happy ending.

Everyone but the baby, that is.

The characters' lives have been altered, enhanced and certainly enriched, literally, by this tiny child. Yet the child is relegated to a less-than-satisfying future. I think the plot was handled better 150 years ago by George Eliot in *Silas Marner*.

This novel, for all its emoting, lacks heart. It seems written by a puppeteer who moves her people in little jerks. Nothing's really at stake, nothing dangerous for the characters.

Still, wanting to see if I was missing something, I went out on an evening of driving rain to see Anna Quindlen herself at a local bookstore. Such is her genuine popularity that more than 150 fans turned out on a dreadful night to hear her read, patiently waiting in cramped conditions while she was half-an-hour late.

Have you ever heard anyone sing "Feelings" as though it was grand opera? That's the way Quindlen reads. She had to tell us that the word "blessings" has a dual meaning in the story.

I began to be fascinated by the whole presentation of literary celebrity. Quindlen is famous for quitting her job as a New York Times columnist to stay home with her children and write novels. She was asked during the question period what is different about writing fiction versus writing a column. Her reply was there is little difference. She learned as a journalist to write "tight," and she found most books too long and indulgent. She said she likes to lead the reader "where he needs to go."

I thought about this. In journalism, you express an opinion or you report the story. You definitely are feeding the reader and there is something tidy about the result.

In fiction, you dream. Novels are large and messy and cannot be too long for those who love them. That's why they are an interesting and life-like art form. In all great novels, there's a point when it seems the author is losing control of the characters and where they are going, much less where the reader is going.

Quindlen writes her own literary epitaph in a passage describing Lydia's favorite novels. "They were foolish books signifying nothing, but they had the appeal of scales played on the piano or multiplication tables recited aloud, a perfect predictability that she had learned unconsciously to love."

R.I.P.

(*Blessings: A Novel* by Anna Quindlen. Random House, 2002. 226 pages)

An artful 'Forgery'
October 11, 2002

> *Oh, what a tangled web we weave,*
> *When first we practice to deceive.*

Sir Walter Scott certainly was not describing the intriguing story told in *The Poet and the Murderer: A True Story of Literary Crime and the Art of Forgery* by Simon Worrall, but his prophetic words fit perfectly. Worrall has taken hold of a complex and interesting subject – forging historic and literary documents – and untangled its many strands to weave a coherent and eye-opening narrative.

This true story might seem impossibly opaque if not for the author's dogged journalistic pursuit of the facts and his ability to construct a plausible chronology and credible motivations of the many people involved.

In 1997, Worrall's interest was piqued when he read that an unpublished poem by Emily Dickinson had been discovered and purchased for the Jones Library in Amherst, Massachusetts. Dan Lombardo, the curator, had raised the necessary $21,000 to bid on this gem at Sotheby's auction house and bring it home with pride. But a further horrid discovery revealed to Lombardo the poem was a fake, a fraud perpetrated by a master forger named Mark Hofmann who was serving a life sentence in Utah for murder.

Lombardo's career could be ruined. His only hope lay in exposing the hoax along with Sotheby's suspected complicity and thereby restoring his reputation.

Worrall takes the reader into the mind and mission of Hofmann, a man of extraordinary talent who as an adolescent began forging rare coins. Raised in the Mormon faith in Salt Lake City, he broke with the church emotionally and intellectually while maintaining a surface compliance. He wanted to exploit the arrogance and weakness he saw in the entrenched hierarchy and rattle the foundations of Mormonism.

Hofmann began to practice the art of forgery, manufacturing documents so seemingly authentic, yet so potentially damaging to the church, that the chief officers paid him huge sums for them, hoping to hide them away. In a period of five years, they bought 450 documents for hundreds of thousands of dollars. Yet Hofmann leaked news of his "discoveries" to the press in devious ways and made fools of the church leaders.

All the while, Hofmann led a placid existence in the Salt Lake community. An upright married man with three children, he set up a laboratory in his basement, mixing chemicals for ink and aging elements for paper. As his reputation as a dealer in rare documents grew, he gained access to the finest library collections and was not above stealing volumes or ripping blank pages from books to use for his forgeries.

He expanded his range. For chump change, he would buy first editions of 19th-century novels and "autograph" them by Mark Twain or Harriet Beecher Stowe. He created "letters" by George Washington, Abraham Lincoln and Daniel Boone.

Hofmann was a clever genius who manipulated people at first for the sheer fun of it. Worrall makes the point that a forger is like an actor, immersing himself in the part, using a "feeling for dialogue and character" to create documents with the "ring of authority." Hofmann's forgeries fooled examiners at the top libraries. Even the FBI could not debunk his work.

In some ways, this part of the story is enticing and Robin Hood-ish. The dazzling creativity of forgery, the exacting research necessary to emulate authenticity is, well, admirable. This man was dedicated and mostly taking advantage of the highly gullible and wealthy people who hang out at Sotheby's or Christie's, trying to impress their friends by owning something important.

I recall so well the hysteria surrounding the sale of Jackie Onassis's personal belongings and the crowds paying thousands of dollars for her wastebaskets. The auction market is big business indeed, driven by hype and supported to the tune of $30 billion a year by people with huge amounts of disposable income.

Worrall's astonishing revelation is that even in this charged and highly voracious atmosphere, getting away with selling phony documents is not that difficult. People want to believe; they want to be told stories. That is the plain truth. They participate in their own deceptions.

Say as a child you had fun-loving parents who carefully placed an old-looking map somewhere for you to "discover," and that map had a big black X marking the spot of buried treasure. If you wanted to believe so much that you went digging, then you understand the wisdom of Worrall's insight.

Hofmann rationalized that if he created a document that was so well done that even experts could not detect the fakery, there was no fraud. So, what's the harm?

I remember an afternoon in the British Museum – the old British Museum – when I pushed aside a blue velvet drape over a locked glass case and peered down at the original manuscript of *Jane Eyre*. The thrill is with me even now: Charlotte Brontë's neat writing, her occasional scratching out of a word, the palpable sense of the moment of creation.

The real scholars – several of whom are the heroes of this book – and the reverence they hold for precious and immortal work, the hours and years they spend toiling away to collect and preserve manuscripts and letters are harmed and mocked by the Hofmanns of the world. Hofmann wanted to make powerful people look stupid, but he snared good and trusting people in his crimes as well.

Hofmann's snarled schemes blew up, literally, as he became more ambitious and desperate for money. Caught in his own many traps, the only way out seemed to be plotting the murder of two men who were squeezing him for payment, threatening him with exposure and bankruptcy.

As skillfully and scientifically as he mixed his forging potions, he constructed bombs and carried out two murders. He was caught and put in prison in 1985. He was 31 years old.

The consequences of his crimes go on. A dozen years later, the Emily Dickinson poem surfaced, auctioned off by the people at Sotheby's who, according to Worrall, knew better. Hofmann is not the only villain here.

Even though Worrall's book is excellent reading, I must note some jarring weaknesses. One unforgivable paragraph compares Hofmann's art to Emily Dickinson's, as though the two were analogous. Also, his lengthy psychological analysis of Dickinson depends on gossip and conjecture, unproven to true Dickinson scholars. He makes a lot of assertions about Dickinson's impenetrable inner life that seem disrespectful. After all, this book has little to do with Dickinson per se, only to the extent that this criminal found it possible to fabricate a poem of hers that fooled a few people for a while. Such was Hofmann's hubris: He thought his poem was better even than some of hers!

Worrall includes facsimiles of the forged poem and a real poem of Dickinson's – a useful display. Read this book for its solid reporting and interesting characters. Skip the passage on Emily's psyche and read one of her poems instead – this one, for instance.

> *Between My Country – and the Others –*
> *There is a Sea –*
> *But Flowers – negotiate between us –*
> *As Ministry.*

(*The Poet and the Murderer: A True Story of Literary Crime and the Art of Forgery* by Simon Worrall. HarperCollins, 2002. 336 pages)

An unforgettable 'Mentor'
October 23, 2002

My Mentor, a shapely and spare book, is Alec Wilkinson's tribute to his friend William Maxwell. It reads more like an exceptional love story than a memoir.

Young writers tend to seek mentors even before they know that is what they need. This is a tenuous and delicate sort of relationship, difficult both to form and describe. Not only writers but countless other beginners yearn for encouragement and praise and for that wiser and more experienced someone to show them what to do.

The business of mentoring can mean anything. These days, a person of superior status "mentors" simply by writing a letter of recommendation or helping a student choose a course of study.

Wilkinson was privy to serious mentoring in the way "primitive fathers taught their sons to stalk, to study tracks, to observe the behavior of their prey, to watch the sky for weather." In other words, Maxwell taught this young man something useful: the "practical and primary" lessons of good writing, how to write dialogue and how to achieve effects upon a reader. This work was done side by side for 15 years, beginning when Wilkinson was 24 and Maxwell was 68.

William Maxwell intended to become an artist, but fate and happenstance intervened and directed him toward a degree in literature and a career as a writer. He backed into a job at The New Yorker – both writing and editing – and just stayed on and on, working and publishing excellent novels.

In his mid-30s, his writer's fog lifted. He courted and married the enchanting and much younger Emily Noyes. This unusual couple enjoyed beauty and prosperity and honored this privilege by using their talents and extending generosity toward others.

After a 55-year marriage of unimaginable happiness – Maxwell found his home to be "uninhabitable" without her – they passed away within eight days of one another in July 2000, when Maxwell was 91 and his precious Emmy was 78.

The actual events of Maxwell's life are unremarkable, but the effect of his work on those who knew him was remarkable indeed. He wrote lasting novels that were not awarded prizes yet were greatly prized by other writers. Wilkinson relates a single episode that speaks volumes about his eminence. "When J. D. Salinger finished *The Catcher in the Rye*, he drove to the Maxwell's house and over the course of an afternoon read it to them on their porch."

While reading his story, I began to think Wilkinson was like a guy who won the lottery. In a way, he did. It's hard not to envy him. At a time of life when he craved attention and direction, when the relationship with his own distant father became troubled, here was Maxwell, his father's best friend, who had the time and desire to teach a young man the practice of good writing, and the affection to go on being his friend until death.

A good editor is a gift to any writer. Just what services an editor performs are somewhat elusive and can be contentious. Wilkinson lauds Maxwell with "understanding what a writer is trying to say and helping him say it if he needs the help." Implied here is a certain modesty and respect – not a bad basis to begin and sustain a relationship.

Part of the attraction between these two men was their delight in one another. They shared an aptitude for hard work and discipline. Wilkinson deftly goes over the ground of why he needed Maxwell and the perils implied by such dependency. He was fortunate that "when it came time to emerge from Maxwell's influence and teaching, we became friends."

Wilkinson also became a terrific writer. This book glows with insight. My habit of turning back tiny triangles on pages worth re-reading pains many true book lovers, the equivalent of nails scratched on a chalkboard. Yet I cannot help it, and when I finished the story of this mentor and pupil, my copy looked like someone had taken a bite from the upper-right-hand corner.

As Maxwell's powers for creative writing declined in later years, when he could no longer sustain the work of long narrative, he literally cut sentences he liked from his paragraphs and stowed them in a folder for future use. I was reminded of Matisse and how he made large cut-outs of dancing shapes when his eyes failed. We can all learn from Maxwell's graceful aging and the way Wilkinson describes his own panic at losing this singular friend.

One feels left out, somehow, being unacquainted with William Maxwell, but because of Alec Wilkinson, he walks off the page. Maxwell taught Wilkinson the value of truth and to make every word count. The student learned well, for I cannot think of one word to cancel or add to this honest and lovely memoir.

(*My Mentor: A Young Man's Friendship with William Maxwell* by Alec Wilkinson. Houghton Mifflin Harcourt, 2002. 192 pages)

A hard working 'Manifesto'
October 31, 2002

With American workers reporting lower job satisfaction than at any time in the past decade, what better time to read *A Working Stiff's Manifesto* by Iain Levison, a man who has worked 42 jobs in 10 years?

I'm not sure why Levison declares this to be a manifesto – a document usually proclaiming intentions or motivations – but putting that aside, his book is for everyone who works. If you are employed and love your job, it will make you more content and perhaps smug. If you are slugging away at something loathsome, it might cause you to reconsider your misfortune. Even if you are unemployed, Levison's travails could make you grateful to be on the greener grass after all.

He is talking about work requiring few skills. A decent haircut and pressed khakis are often enough to get you hired, or being able to start that afternoon. Levison is an itinerant worker, drifting among available jobs, always looking for something better. Comparing himself to Tom Joad of *The Grapes of Wrath*, he jokes that the only difference is Joad did not blow $40,000 getting a degree in English.

The plan was to work awhile and then write The Great American Novel, but somewhere along the way, Levison kind of lost the plot. Instead, he fell into the slough of living paycheck-to-paycheck, scraping by, accumulating few possessions, ready to move on at a moment's notice.

Levison iterates his various jobs with smart aleck sarcasm and profane wit. A brief stint as a gopher for a movie shoot is truly hilarious and scathingly revealing of that stereotypically glamorous world. His powers of observation as he moves about the workplace provide lively narrative. This book is never boring.

Let's see, from being a fish cutter for a gourmet food store, he segues to a job as bartender for a Scarsdale socialite and then drives a truck filling oil tanks for rich customers along Philadelphia's Main Line. From there, he goes on to paint garages and perform illegal cable hook-ups for an entire neighborhood before landing steady work cooking in a chain restaurant. The list goes on.

Why so many jobs? Sometimes Levison gets fired for clumsy mistakes or "attitude" or simply because of seasonal lay-offs. Mostly, he gets bored or tired and quits in the face of low pay and Scroogy employers. I must say, the man is not afraid of hard physical labor and seems to enjoy his strong and healthy body.

He lugs furniture for a moving company and, in the longest sustained section, flies to Alaska to make a killing in the seafood industry. This consists of standing 16 hours a day on the "slime line" gutting fish. In order to increase his earnings, Levison signs a contract for three trips on a fishing vessel and goes to sea for higher wages. One of his assignments is to stand in a pit onboard and have live mackerel or perch dumped on him, neck-deep, which he then must shovel or kick into a tunnel.

Unbelievably, there is something more awful. After four days on a nasty crabbing boat, Levison realizes he "managed to find something that combines everything unpleasant in life with a low paycheck." Very low, he finds out. He is guaranteed a percentage of the catch, but the crew is not catching any crabs.

I cannot imagine a more definitive statement of what it's like to bottom-fish the social strata. Levison shows what work is – applying for jobs you don't care about, filling out endless forms no one will read, taking drug tests only for regulations – not because anyone cares – and being faked into attending "seminars" that are come-ons for multi-level marketing schemes. He refers to his English degree as a "$40,000 fly-swatter" and adds that in many cases, it's actually a deterrent to employment.

A few paragraphs describe moments of luminous relief. Many of these jobs require dormitory living with strangers in cramped situations. Unspeakable food is offered as part of the package, luring workers into thinking they are getting a great deal. In this atmosphere, a rare interlude of privacy or a hot shower or clean clothes becomes absurdly poetic and sensual.

I kept thinking of *The Cliff Walk*, Don Snyder's interesting account a few years back of his fall from being a college professor to learning how to be a competent house painter in a cruel job market. The poignancy of Snyder's story hinged on being a family man and having many mouths to feed in addition to his own. Levison seems blissfully free to come and go and though he frequently and obviously longs for female companionship, he does not whine about missing relationships.

I liked his description of working for a trucker named Jim and the miseries of that business. Jim calls himself an "independent contractor" and Levison remarks it just means nobody is paying for your health insurance. Levison is clever but this volume does not begin to approach George Orwell's *Down and Out in Paris* for real social commentary on the underclass. He lacks the range for biting satire, being content to make a few wisecracks but leave a lot of potentially rich material scattered along the roadside.

Still, on its own merits, this book speaks about people we often don't want to think about. I read in The Washington Post recently that 8,000 hotel employees will lose their jobs before Christmas because rooms are not being booked. You think you are working toward a career of sorts and then it's all over.

Levison's youth and sass provide a bouncy sub-text to his stories. Although he recounts some pretty depressing scenes – the manager of a bug-spray company with his dirty wall bearing a single pathetic plaque honoring him as top salesman 10 years ago – you somehow want to laugh. Yet there is always a somber message of desperate people scrambling to attain or cling to meaningless jobs, often wasting their wages, just because they can. It's the one power they have.

Levison introduces many colorful characters and occasionally realizes he'll miss them when he moves on. I think I'll miss

Levison. I wonder what he will do when he grows up. This book is a good start.

(*A Working Stiff's Manifesto: A Memoir* by Iain Levison. Soho Press, 2002. 164 pages)

Not 'Crazed' after all
November 8, 2002

It is amazing that one of the finest prose-stylists in America today is a Chinese émigré who once fought in Mao's army.

After coming here on a student visa and painstakingly teaching himself to write in English, Ha Jin went on to win the National Book Award. With his new novel, ironically titled *The Crazed*, he has surpassed even the excellent standard he set a few years back with the dazzling debut of *Waiting*.

I was such an admirer of *Waiting* that I hesitated a moment before opening the beautiful, slightly textured cover of *The Crazed*. Sometimes, second efforts are massive letdowns. Yet Jin does not disappoint. He delivers a deeper, bolder and certainly more dramatic work that rewards a patient reader with a huge literary pay-off.

The delicate yet powerful story unfolds in the provincial university town of Shanning. It is the spring of 1989, and students are demonstrating in Beijing for democratic representation against a repressive regime. In this backwater, where few people seem to notice or care what is going on in the capital, the eminent Professor Yang has suffered a stroke. Considered a great teacher, poet, translator of Brecht, he lies in an inadequate hospital room, given to helpless ravings, his mind now resembling "a broken safe

– all the valuables stored in it were scattered around helter-skelter."

The story is told by Jian Wan, a 26-year-old graduate student who is engaged to Yang's daughter, Meimei. Meimei is studying for a medical degree in Beijing while Jian remains stuck in Shanning, preparing for his qualifying exams for a doctoral degree in comparative literature. He hopes to join Meimei in Beijing where they will study and eventually go abroad to work.

The real love story develops as Jian tends his father-in-law-to-be. Every afternoon, he bicycles under "the scalding sun, the asphalt street turned doughy" to watch over this slowly deteriorating genius. Jian crams for his upcoming tests, staring at Japanese flash cards and listening all the while to the man's lunatic delirium.

From Yang's spewing of random nonsense – unconnected bits of poetry, memories, furious denunciations – certain themes emerge. Yang laments unrequited affairs in the past and the current frustrations of departmental quibbling. He rages that his life has been pointless – scholars are mere clerks – and most of all worries he is "not worthy of my suffering."

Jian listens intently. Yang has occasional lucid periods. The young student begins to question his own choices, whether he truly wishes to follow the path of academia that his dear professor now condemns as "just a play of words and sophistries ... no original ideas, only platitudes." Jian wishes to live a more useful life, an active life, so that "at the final hour I could feel fulfillment and contentment" and not die in demented agony.

How to manage this in a culture where petty officials run everyone's lives, from Party-assigned housing to the logistics of marriage to choosing professions becomes tortured conflict for Jian. Letters from Meimei constantly describe the rising discord in Beijing as students confront the People's Liberation Army, who are supposed to protect the citizens, not attack them. Meimei won't get involved in politics. She is appalled when Jian, falling behind in his studies, decides not to sit for his exams. To her, that is his only ticket out of Shanning.

Another conflict is Jian's growing attachment to Weiya, a lovely colleague who also comes to visit Professor Yang. An artist, struggling to break out of the choking academic system, Weiya at one time almost became a lover to Yang. She is one of a dozen or so characters who flesh out this narrative with their stories of endurance and even hopefulness in a system crushing to the spirit. The author displays a deft touch with his people, taking his time, polishing his sentences so that there is loveliness even in graphic descriptions of human misery.

As Jian wavers in Hamlet-like indecision during the stifling summer, pondering his situation and slowly realizing he has been manipulated by various malevolent forces, the range of this author's extraordinary talent grows more impressive. Few writers since Jane Austen have depicted better the languid intensity of inner life, of living in a restricted class culture where rules dominate and there is little privacy. Speaking openly is forbidden or so dangerous that much guessing must go on. I cannot imagine Elizabeth Bennett or Marianne Dashwood facing greater peril than Weiya if her affair with Yang is exposed. A girl losing her virtue is branded "a little broken shoe."

Jian learns well the final clear and brilliant lessons his teacher has to offer. The sluggishness of the sick room gives way and the pace crescendos as the clash in Beijing grows deadly. Almost by happenstance, Jian travels there in time to witness the slaughter of civilians and innocents in Tiananmen Square. In shock and now labeled a "counterrevolutionary," Jian returns to Shanning and certain arrest.

He is tormented by a vision of China "in the form of an old hag so decrepit and brainsick that she would devour her children to sustain herself. Insatiable, she had eaten many tender lives before, was gobbling new flesh and blood now, and would surely swallow more." Jian resolutely escapes to an ambiguous future – but one of free choice – in a page-turning climax.

It is not surprising that Ha Jin's work is unpublished in his native country. Yet in the soil that nurtured this fine and exciting writer and incubated a passion and love for words, we find a gift to America and world literature. This sane and elegant novel is anything but crazed.

(*The Crazed* by Ha Jin. Pantheon Books, 2002. 323 pages)

Won't Quite 'Take You There'
November 15, 2002

Joyce Carol Oates is a formidable presence in the literary world, so prolific a writer that it is difficult to evaluate her in the usual ways. Her body of work stands like a Devil's Tower risen on the plain, an object of awe, never eroding, constantly ascending.

Oates has produced novels, plays, poetry, even young adult works and perennially makes the short list for Nobel Prize consideration. She publishes so often that for a while – like Stephen King using a pseudonym – she also wrote under the name Rosamond Smith. This frail-looking woman astonishes us all. She runs miles every day, keeps up a rigorous teaching schedule at Princeton and even does her own housework.

Oates is definitely the Energizer Bunny of American literature. Reading one of her novels – say her latest, *I'll Take You There* – is to experience a sort of channeling. It's as though you see a stranger on the Metro one day and idly wonder: What is her story?

Then a book lands with a thud on your doorstep that tells you everything this person has ever seen, done, thought, eaten, worn or read. A river of words flows about this character – who her grandparents are, what they eat for Sunday dinner, what jobs did she have while still in junior high, how much she paid for a used sweater – until as a reader you are almost gasping, "Stop! Please stop! Too much information!"

The central figure of this first-person narrative does not reveal her name. An eccentric young woman searching for her identity, she inexplicably joins the sorority Kappa Gamma Pi at Syracuse University in the early 1960s, an act she later terms "impetuous, infatuated, unexamined." Seeking sisters, seeking connection, she is admitted because of her brilliance and the hope she will raise the Kappas' grade point average.

Yet this troubled heroine is so out of place in the grand house and the totalitarian Greek system she suffers a brilliantly depicted breakdown. Not since Sylvia Plath wrote *The Bell Jar* has mental suffering by an artistic misfit been so poignantly explored.

She is "de-activated" and, in the central section of the novel, becomes attracted to the voice of Vernor Matheius, a graduate student in philosophy. Vernor's is a "voice of seduction, a voice of pleading. A voice of logic, reason, conviction. A voice like a caress." Vernor is black. This is the '60s so Vernor is still referred to as a Negro, and the girl, who now calls herself by the made-up name of Anellia, by her own nomenclature becomes a Negro-lover.

Although Anellia is desperately lonely and somewhat drawn to those of outcast status, Vernor's exotic color is not the basis for attraction. The lovers are suffused with philosophy. They repair to the campus pub to discuss Schopenhauer's triumph of the Will. They need to analyze every action and thought a hundred times, to use philosophy as "an ice pick ... a surgical instrument for analysis, dissection, debridement, and comprehension." Dozens of German and Greek philosophers are quoted – Nietzsche, Wittgenstein, Plato – their thoughts blending with those of the couple who, like Spinoza, will "analyze the actions and appetites of men as if it were a question of lines, of planes, and of solids."

Love is a trap and another path to madness for Anellia. She comes to believe that "the unexamined life, the life that's led without a continuous self-scrutiny ... was madness."

Back to excessive self-examination, to exhausting details – six pages to describe sour lovemaking; 12 pages when it is excellent – a piling up of moments that leads this young woman at last to sanity and connection with – Ah! – herself!

Oates's characters never seem quite normal, yet they are believable and real. Finishing this novel, I felt informed and as usual in total thrall to this author's great mind and her ability to carry me through to the end. Yet sometimes, at the end of a book, I want to be in love. I crave a perfume lingering in the air and a metaphorical pillow to hug. After all, I've invested many hours in this story and I want a warm reward. But warmth is missing and because of that I cannot get passionate about Oates. I settle for admiration and respect. It is as though she has made me exercise.

Philosophers try to prove their theories by pure rationality, reasoning and logic. If *I'll Take You There* is a long philosophical proof, Oates proves her case. Her heroine breaks out of her false paths and finds truth in self and writing. In so doing, she tells you everything -- Everything! – what career Vernor ends up in 20 years later, how much she pays for her VW Beetle and how much she gets in resale. At the end, nothing is left for the reader to wonder about, except perhaps to ponder how Joyce Carol Oates does this, time after time after time.

(*I'll Take You There* by Joyce Carol Oates. Ecco, 2002. 290 pages)

Don't be a 'Stranger'
November 22, 2002

Deborah Mathis is a syndicated columnist and a familiar face on television commentary shows. She has an appealing wit and comfortable speaking style. She is quick to count her blessings and thank her God, "who has been ridiculously good to me all of my days." She is blessed with the talent to write. *Yet a Stranger* is an articulate and provocative book on a tricky subject: racism.

Mathis recounts a litany of shameful grievances against blacks in America – the slights and indignities, the "Look" of disdain and distrust, the inequities and atrocities visited upon people of color. She reminds us of painful headlines of senseless deaths on the New Jersey Turnpike, the killing of Amadou Diallo, wrongful accusations by Charles Stuart and Susan Smith of being attacked by "a black person." These examples are cringing to recall, but they read here as mildly repetitive. When Mathis adds her personal stories of suffering from prejudice, she somehow sounds more original and interesting.

One original idea is using the notion of "home" to shape and drive her narrative. Home is both a concept and reality we build for ourselves. "I believe I speak for the masses," she writes, "when I say that black Americans are ready to relax and be at home in America. And to ask, when will America welcome us?"

In this statement lies her conundrum. No doubt that racism exists. Mathis could cut her examples in half and still have ample condemning evidence. But does she speak "for the masses" when she declares the problems existing today are all because whites are inhospitable to blacks? For that is her message, repeated in every chapter. "We" are a maligned yet wonderful deserving people and "you" are the cause of all our societal problems.

By assuming the editorial "we," as she does throughout, Mathis has loaded a lot onto her plate. She denies the validity of black voices that disagree with hers – such as Ward Connerly, who fervently opposed affirmative action in California, labeling him "a black man, at least in appearance." She writes in sweeping generalities, extolling the old days of "black community, when we belonged to one another " when blacks felt "at ease ... thanks to the industry and will of black entrepreneurs and good neighbors." Children were happy and protected in that community. She relates a history of desegregation breaking up this loving community and setting people adrift. This all rings true but it is a sore point with not just black people. Daniel Moynihan studied and wrote vigorously about the loss of those communities.

It is undeniable that Americans have struggled with race issues since pre-Colonial times. Progress is slow and Mathis, correctly, is impatient for results. Yet she refuses to count results when they do appear. Rather, she sets up an unhelpful "we" vs. "them" slugfest. Blacks who have achieved great success and stature – Tiger Woods, for example – do not receive her approbation. If he were not so pleasing to whites, she asserts, he would not be the "darling of the sports world."

In her opinion, white attitude represses blacks, keeps them from achieving and from enjoying the full fruits and benefits of what life in America has to offer.

I frequently found myself cheering the strong confident voice of Mathis. She speaks proudly of her color, her heritage and, frankly, her good mind. I know she is right.

Mathis looks solidly at that past, more skeptically at the present. Even though I applaud her, at the same time I resent that she gives no credit to whites who have climbed that learning curve of injustice. I cannot change the color of my skin any more than she can, but as a member of an ethnically and racially mixed extended family I know how I feel and think about these issues. It definitely is not "us" vs. "them." How can one think blacks are terrorized only by whites when we have recently experienced the Washington-area sniper attacks? Lines constantly blur and change occurs as fast as cloud shadows race across the prairie.

If Mathis still does not feel "at home" in America, I wonder where her spirit is residing. She ends her book with suggestions for improving the lot of blacks, including guarding the children, creating networks to pool resources, connecting with God and civic and political activism. These are excellent ideas, but they are excellent for all citizens, regardless of color.

Mathis has taken on a huge and complex subject. She obviously has many complaints about the country we live in. I ultimately came to believe she needed to get this out of her system and can now write a better book, one that sounds less scolding in tone and combative with whites. I would love to read something by her that is more about her particular and "ridiculously" good experiences.

Yet a Stranger activated many thoughts and memories in me. I took scads of notes, reacting verbally and viscerally, at times churning emotionally. I thought of my cousin Judy, a fabulous individual, an artist and also black. She has endured many affronts while making unforgettable contributions to young people and the world. Judy once told me she brushed off the snubs like so many cockroaches – she proceeded to make elegant flicking motions, like the poised and graceful dancer she is.

It is my impression that Deborah Mathis has chosen to carry around a lot of cockroaches. I wish we could sit and talk, perhaps argue back and forth and have a few laughs. I would like to think she would feel welcome in my home.

(*Yet a Stranger: Why Black Americans Still Don't Feel at Home* by Deborah Mathis. Warner Books, 2002. 258 pages)

Travel as 'Art'
November 29, 2002

Herman Melville sent Ishmael off on the cruise of a lifetime because of "a damp, drizzly November" in his soul. I know the feeling. In this particular November, it has rained nearly every day, snow and sleet are in the forecast, and because there are no triple digits in my checkbook and the holidays are approaching, I am not likely to be winging off to some island or remote but charming village.

So I pick up *The Art of Travel* by Alain de Botton and read, "If our lives are dominated by a search for happiness, then perhaps few activities reveal as much about the dynamics of this quest ... than our travels." Thus begins a delightful armchair journey, a most satisfying surrogate for an actual voyage.

I became addicted to Botton's voice a few years back when I read *How Proust Can Change Your Life*. I have since re-read that book twice and find its traits of wit and sense to be just what one desires in a close friend. This current volume displays a similar ability of the author to act as a companion or chum who shares stimulating and lively intimacies with you. One finishes *The Art of Travel* determined to live in a more conscious and aware manner.

Jacques Barzun said the book, like the bicycle, is a perfect form. The first thing one notices is the user-friendly shape of *Travel* – almost square and pocket-sized with a leather-like binding. Just holding it gives pleasure. Black and white photos and reproductions of paintings accompany the text exactly where they are discussed in the narrative.

Botton begins by describing the giddy anticipation of setting off for a destination – in this case, a trip to Barbados with a friend – and the ensuing difficulties of letting go of worries long enough to enjoy oneself. Planning and expectation alone do not allow happiness in longed-for places. In what could pass for Paradise, Botton and his friend get into a roiling spat over a crème caramel that ruins at least one day. This is hilarious to read and conjures up similar memories in my own mental scrapbook but the episode points up a difficulty of truly getting away just by going to a different address.

I let Botton lead me on walking tours of Amsterdam, the Lake District of England and ancient Madrid. Along the way, he chatters about architecture, artists, Flaubert in Egypt and why it took the English so long to appreciate the beauty of their own country. I could listen to this forever. He speaks of French dukes and early explorers as though they were personal friends of his, people he wants me to know.

I love learning about Baudelaire's influence on the American artist Edward Hopper. It seems Baudelaire experienced an unhappy childhood and propelled himself, as he wrote, "anywhere! anywhere! so long as it is out of the world!" Wow! Though he spent a life on the move writing about ships, clouds and trains, he never quite resolved the ambivalence of both wanting to be away and seeking a home.

What inspired Hopper, another soul who "failed to find a home in the ordinary world," was Baudelaire's attention to places of departure and waiting – terminals and stations and half-empty rooms. Botton explicates several of Hopper's paintings that evoke this sensibility of stops-along-the-way, of figures sitting in all-night coffee shops or in a train compartment, expressing a stillness while in motion. He shows me why these solitary people are not especially lonely and to appreciate better both wandering and art.

A passage on John Ruskin teaches something of lasting value – how to hold on to the beauty we find in our travels. Ruskin, helped by his indulgent and fond parents, began traveling early in life, developing an exquisite appreciation for the beauty of nature.

"Beauty is fugitive," Botton instructs us. "We find it in places to which we may never return." There are ways of capturing those moments of light or season, perhaps taking a photo or scribbling words in a journal.

Ruskin, who became one of our greatest writers on art, believed one could literally possess beauty by "consciously understanding what we have loved." He taught people how to draw to see better, to possess in ways that only creative involvement could satisfy. I become so inspired reading this I decide to include a tiny sketchpad the next time I go anywhere!

Probably the least successful section is Botton venturing on a walking tour of the Sinai Desert. He tries to make a case for fathoming the sublime in vast spaces, recounting tribulations from the Book of Job. I'm not sure much more needs to be said of the desert beyond what David Lean depicted in "Lawrence of Arabia" or Paul Bowles wrote in *The Sheltering Sky*. Happily, this is a brief detour and then we are back in Arles, France, tracking down Van Gogh's cypress trees and orange skies.

I disagree with Botton that ordinary airline food is somehow tastier and more exciting because of the clouds outside the window. But I agree with almost all his other opinions, such as, "What we find exotic abroad may be what we hunger for in vain at home," and that "Difference alone is not enough to elicit pleasure, or not for long. The difference has to seem like an improvement." How true, and something I shall remember if I am ever again at Disney World.

I share with Botton a fondness for staring at the homes of strangers and imagining a perfectly contented life for myself behind utterly unfamiliar doors. And my heart also picks up a beat when I see unknown words on signs, wonderful words he repeats like "aankomst" and "uitgang." In fact, that's another thing I like about this book, Botton's use of "car park" and "kerb" and "learnt." He is English, after all, and this usage lends a touch of spice and novelty to his tales.

"Journeys are the midwives of thought," Botton writes, "helped along by the flow of landscape." He reminds me of why, when my brain cannot come unstuck from some fret or worrisome problem, getting in the car and just driving for a couple of hours often helps toward crafting a solution. Also, he tells me clever ways of traveling by simply staying at home. Because that seems to be my lot at present, this is a valuable book indeed. In keeping with the season, I am not only delighted with but even thankful for *The Art of Travel.*"

(*The Art of Travel* by Alain de Botton. Pantheon Books, 2002. 249 pages)

Odyssey from 'East' to 'West'
December 9, 2002

In the confusing aftermath of September 11, I received an email – one of those "FWD" messages one often deletes unread. For some reason, I opened this one and became instantly drawn to its unique voice. The voice spoke with passion and reason, explaining the reality of the situation, imploring me to understand the difference between the repressive Taliban and the suffering people of Afghanistan.

In those shattering days, here were strength and refreshing clarity. It is trite to say the words electrified me, but they really did during the initial numbing hours. Although the words arrived from a stranger, it seemed like a letter from an unmet friend.
The email was signed Tamim Ansary, a name almost unknown until millions of people eventually received the remarkable

"FWD." It turns out Ansary is a middle-aged Afghan-American living in San Francisco. He unwittingly sent his message to a few friends who then multiplied recipients through the magic of the Internet. I now know this because of his lovely and at times heartbreaking memoir *West of Kabul, East of New York*, in which he fleshes out the story of his youth in Afghanistan and later emigration to the United States.

I found the book on a table at Kramerbooks & Afterwords Café, on Dupont Circle in Washington. A young boy's face looked up at me from the cover photograph. He appears to be around 9 or 10. On his head is elaborate headgear wrapped somewhat haphazardly. In the center perches a soft white dove-like bird. The boy's mouth is not visible, but his shining black eyes stare at me so playfully, I just know he is wearing a big grin.

This captivating photo is not of the author but inspired cover art. It doesn't matter. The picture perfectly embodies the spirit of the book – a boy gazing at the world with curiosity, wonder and humor. You want to know him and, fortunately, this articulate book satisfies that desire.

Ansary, a wonderful storyteller, is gifted with an unusual story to tell, beginning with his Afghan father meeting a young Finnish-American woman while studying in Chicago in the 1940s. He wore stylish suits and "snazzy" hats and she "didn't consider herself pretty," but the two of them discovered they could tango together – literally. They married and moved to Kabul to live and raise their three children.

In this first section, Ansary describes his boyhood in poetic and informative language. His family lived in a house inside a compound surrounded by nine-foot walls. Other relatives had their own houses within these walls. The city itself was made up of hundreds of such compounds where families lived intricate and connected lives, moving about and interacting, always together. I picture a vast city of family farms, each with a self-contained life, exotic and fascinating.

As Ansary tells it, in this communal atmosphere, the concept of personal privacy was almost unknown. Yet he was free and protected, roaming with his many cousins and friends, an idyllic life for a boy. Because Ansary is such a good writer, I understand at last what family means to Afghans, how deeply they are rooted in that soil and why the ancestral village is so important.

Ansary always understood the dual nature of his heritage. He and his siblings did not eat with their fingers from the communal dishes as did his relatives – rather, they used forks and spoons. When he was on the verge of adolescence, his family moved to the tiny town of Lashkargah where his father, a government official, helped manage a huge Afghan/American project of transforming the wasted Helmand Valley into fertile land. During his six years there, Ansary lived what he calls a "quasi-American life."

His father's rank at this outpost commanded privileges and allowed his mother to enjoy parties and social life. In many ways, this period became the happiest ever for the family. Then political forces altered his father's situation and young Ansary found himself back in Kabul at the age of 16, smarting with humiliation. The visible sign of the family's demotion in rank was being issued an ugly Soviet Volga to drive instead of the Mercedes given to higher officials.

Always a good student, he applied to and was accepted at the Colorado Rocky Mountain School in Carbondale. The family emigrated to the States with Ansary, but this began a process of division. Later, his father returned to Afghanistan alone, choosing his large extended family there over his small nuclear one in America.

The late William Maxwell, a fine writer and editor at The New Yorker, once said: "Write as if you wish to be understood by an unusually bright 10-year-old."

This exactly denotes Ansary's style. Woven into his stories are lucid explanations of Islam, the history of Afghanistan, the heroes of his youth, what school was like in bare classrooms with no books, how women lived, the joys and cruelties of Islamic society – all of it highly educational and absolutely painless to absorb. In addition to "speaking" beautifully, this author is capable of painting large colorful canvases with his words.

The middle section of the book finds a thoroughly Americanized Ansary emerging from the counterculture of the '60s to begin his true adult life as a writer. His family has scattered – his mother teaching in Maryland, his sister Rebecca living in Pennsylvania and his younger brother Riaz reaching back to the Islamic way of life. Ansary clashes with Riaz about specific brutal practices of Islam, causing a painful rift. Although raised in Islam and even speaking of the Prophet Muhammad as "a really great guy ... a regular guy," the author has drifted far from his childhood religion.

Everything changes again. The Ayatollah Khomeini takes over the government of Iran, Americans are held hostage, Ansary meets Debby Krant, the love of his life, and sets off on assignment for Pacific News Service to report on the causes of Islamic fundamentalism. He has the vague goal of reaching Pakistan and perhaps seeing his father again. This journey from Tangier to Morocco, Algeria and Turkey is full of tense border crossings, losing money from foolish mistakes and backtracking. His exhausting effort to become a "macho journalist" and explain cultures in turmoil is just amazing. Although he never does write the story or reach his geographic destination, Ansary has the courage to portray himself in all his gullibility and inexperience.

He ends up is a Paris hotel room reading *The Odyssey* and yearning for a return to Debby – his own Penelope.

What he does achieve is a grasp of who he is and how at last to integrate his cross-cultural background into a fully mature life. Deciding "the Islamic world is someone else's, not mine," he returns home to "take up my life as one unconflicted soul: Tamim Ansary, American guy." Yet he also found ways to understand his now deceased father, to reconcile with his brother and connect culturally with the growing Afghan community in California.

When September 11 occurred, with all the love inside him for his country of birth and his country of choice, he fired off an e-mail heard round the world. The book closes with the text of that e-mail and, reading it again, I marveled at the density of thought and the economy of his few potent words. He asked if the West had the stomach to go against Osama bin Laden.

I read an article the other day in The Washington Post about the situation in Kabul today. It sounds light years away from the sweet family compounds of Ansary's youth, where uncles sat around endlessly reciting family history. Now the streets are crammed with vehicles and construction goes on round the clock. Expatriate Afghans are flowing back into the ravaged country, earnestly trying to fix up homes and build schools. Slick entrepreneurs try to make a quick buck as many thousands wonder how to make it through the bitterly cold winter.

Tamim Ansary taught me much about his country and its generous, warm people who love music, the spoken word and ancient kinship. His book is one that stays with you, coloring the way you look at bright-eyed boys or listen to the news and think about this world.

(*West of Kabul, East of New York: An Afghan American Story* by Tamim Ansary. Farrar, Straus and Giroux, 2002. 292 pages)

A lingering 'Afterglow'
December 12, 2002

"It was Saturday night and we had a date." So begins *Afterglow*, Francis Davis' all-too-brief account of his last real conversation with Pauline Kael. Oh, how I envy him! Imagine! An actual date with Pauline Kael – to see a movie, of course.

From the 1960s until her retirement in 1991, Kael reigned as "the queen bee of American movie critics" at The New Yorker magazine. As a young man, Davis became a fan of Kael's writing. He sent her a copy of his first published book – a collection of essays about jazz – requesting a blurb. She readily complied. From a shared love of film and good writing grew a friendship lasting until Kael's death from Parkinson's disease on September 3, 2001.

Not long before that date, Kael sat down with Davis to record this interesting chat about her life and her opinions about movies and the current culture. She seems as bright and quick as in her prime when legions of loyal fans, myself included, waited eagerly for her next review.

When someone achieves the status of Pauline Kael, it is natural to ask why she was so great and arguably the most influential critic of her time – and perhaps ever.

A reasonable proof would be simply to read her collected works. Davis makes the case that "No one else has written as vividly about movies, or about the experience of seeing movies." Lore surrounding the diminutive Kael rumbles with admiration and laughter about how physically involved she became while watching a movie. Laughing, rocking in her seat, talking to the screen were all part of the experience for her. She viewed intensely, completely and retained almost perfect recall of what she had seen. She never saw films more than once, a fact amazing to film buffs. She couldn't understand why anyone would want to see something twice.

Reading Davis's book convinced me Kael's greatness lay in the fact that she absolutely loved films and would write for nothing and cared not at all for others' opinions of her opinions. She possessed a sureness in her own point of view developed rather early in her life when she ran a repertory cinema in San Francisco and wrote up program notes.

Over the years and after she became famous, she was offered teaching positions at several universities, but the academic life was not for her. She couldn't "face it," even though it provided a secure living, which writing did not. Her chosen path "was insane financially," she said, describing how she wrote constantly for magazines and only earned a few hundred a year. Yet she did not wish to "write academic English in an attempt to elevate movies, because I think that actually lowers them."

"I loved writing," she told Davis. "I really loved the gamble of writing, the risk-taking. I loved the speed of it, the fact that you had your say and moved on to something else." That was the reason she hated Hollywood when she tried working there. "Nothing was ever over and done with. You would nag over the same material endlessly."

Kael found her perfect world during her 30 years at The New Yorker. She was speedy, cranking out weekly reviews and opinion pieces. She really got it, the love affair of America with the movies, and she helped foster and intensify that love. She had the knack of discovering truly great films, not what we call today blockbusters, but important work needing a push to get it before the public, Just about single-handedly, she turned "Last Tango in Paris" into a huge hit. And when she decided to send a valentine to Cary Grant, well, he became the subject of her legendary essay "The Man from Dream City."

On the other hand, no one could be more cutting than Kael – such as her description of Dyan Cannon "looking a bit like Lauren Bacall and a bit like Jeanne Moreau, but the wrong bits." Cannon laughed it off. Kael's motive was not vicious ruination. She simply wrote as she thought and spoke, with clarity and honesty and she seemed always to be right.

It's just a fact that when one reads someone regularly, especially a writer with a voice as singular as Kael's, one forms a kind of friendship. I miss her. I know I can always pull one of her books off the shelf and re-read her reviews and essays, but it's wonderful to have the fresh material in this book. I'm glad to know she stayed vital to the end, watching movies through the miracle of videos when she could no longer go out to a theater.

One of the delicious pleasures of this book is to find out at last what she thought of certain more recent films. She loved "Three Kings." Yes! I wrote in the margin. She called "American Beauty" "heavy and turgid." Another exclamation point! She would not even go to see "Gladiator." Thank you, Pauline!

It turns out she did not retire from The New Yorker strictly because of illness. Rather, she quite suddenly could not go on writing about terrible movies, and movies were becoming so bad. "I love writing about movies when I can discover something in them – when I can get something out of them that I can share with people," she told Davis.

She left the darkened theater and largely kept her thoughts from her public. I really felt the loss of her special light. Davis gives some of that back to us in this very welcome *Afterglow*.

(*Afterglow: A Last Conversation with Pauline Kael* by Francis Davis. DaCapo Press, 2002. 126 pages)

A concise 'Churchill'
December 18, 2002

John Keegan's biography of Winston Churchill weighs in at under 200 pages and seems positively meteoric compared to the usual heavy tomes deemed necessary to recount long and productive lives. Yet this brilliant little book illuminates the life and career of one of the most important men of the 20th century and tells a sweeping story in a way that is richly gratifying.

Keegan clears the furniture out of the room and allows us to see the bare bones and structure of Churchill's amazing and somewhat improbable life. Here was a sickly boy, the son of an English lord and beautiful American mother who was neglected in ways by both. Unimpressive in his studies, he nevertheless became a great and courageous soldier, the leading orator and writer of history of his time.

I don't know why, but I had forgotten until Keegan reminded me that Churchill won the Nobel Prize for Literature in 1953. Although he barely passed his exams to be accepted into Sandhurst, the British military academy, he did some things extremely well. One of those was to master the English sentence. When he joined the 4th Hussars in India, with time on his hands, he read deeply into history, especially Edward Gibbon's "Decline and Fall of the Roman Empire."

As he became involved in battles and skirmishes, he sent dispatches and articles to newspapers, supplementing his scant wages. Thus, journalism, war and a later segue into politics blended the themes of his life.

Keegan begins with his own belated discovery of Churchill's power of language and follows with a thrilling narration of the young officer's baptism in war and display of personal courage. Churchill developed an early certainty in his ability to judge military situations, which stood him well in the turbulent years leading up to World War II. It would be wonderful to think careers progressed smoothly from early success to mature leadership to distinguished old age. Such was not the case here. Although Churchill was unafraid to test himself and he had limitless faith in his powers to lead, his path was one of success followed by disappointment, retreat and "black dog" depression, leading again to fresh challenge and triumph.

The key to his epic resurgence time and again was his possession of, as Keegan calls it, "remarkable resilience." When he was defeated in an election, when his spendthrift habits rampaged and the creditors were hounding him, when his fellow members of Parliament turned away from him with scorn, when no one would listen to his warnings of rising Nazism in Germany, "somehow he swam rather than sank."

During the times he was unwanted in government leadership positions, he worked diligently on his books, his painting, or on his estate and waited for his next moment.

The great moment arrived May 10, 1940, when he was called as prime minister. For five years, he led his countrymen through "their darkest hours," constantly repeating the words to encourage dampened spirits and flagging hearts – "hardship and agony, but also sunshine and hope and the promise eventually of conquest and victory."

For Churchill never allowed himself to speak of defeat or appeasement or accommodation with Hitler. From the beginning of the war, his only goal was winning.

He articulated his will to win in a series of immortal speeches that commanded the attention of the world. CBS Radio reporter Edward R. Murrow said Churchill "mobilized the English language and sent it into battle." These "tools of battle" literally lifted the moral tone of the war to the highest ideals of liberty and humanity. His words sustained his people and inspired them when nations all over Europe were falling to Nazi invasion.

Whenever Keegan quotes Churchill in his fighting form, familiar as the phrases may be – "conquer we must, conquer we shall" – the thrill has not faded. One sees again, as in a thousand books and films, the courage and tenacity of besieged citizens. After the war, Churchill did not take the credit, rather gave it to the people, telling them it was their victory. And so it was, but one man embodied the spirit leading to that tremendous victory.

In Keegan's view, the "glow of military achievement and the splendor of empire have almost faded away, but a true glory continues to gleam over Churchill's life, works and words." This book certainly adds to that glory and keeps this personal history from dulling with age.

I admire the economy and artistry of this work, It is part of, and a splendid example of, a series called Penguin Lives, edited primarily by James Atlas. These biographies are small and intimate in nature, giving the essence of a life, the important details and not necessarily all the clutter. When I was a child, I loved those little orange biographies of famous Americans, still cherished and collected by many. They were so readable, with elegant silhouette illustrations of their subjects: Dolley Madison, Jane Addams, Thomas Edison.

This Penguin series is like an adult version of those earlier books. I've enjoyed Larry McMurtry writing about Crazy Horse, Edmund White on Marcel Proust and Karen Armstrong on the Buddha. One unfortunate entry was Jane Smiley's "Charles Dickens," but I can't wait for the promise of Bobbie Ann Mason doing Elvis.

Keegan writing about Winston Churchill is a perfect match. Keegan enjoys the same conversational style anchored by solid scholarship that distinguishes Churchill's books. In these troubled and uncertain times, reading his brisk review of menace and tyrants of the past, of elevated rhetoric leading to victory and one genuine hero is like giving a gift to oneself.

(*Winston Churchill* by John Keegan. Viking, 2002. 208 pages)

Showing us 'How to Be Alone'
January 14, 2003

Jonathan Franzen is credited or despised (by the People Who Care About Such Things) for the demise of Oprah's Book Club. That might or might not be the case. Perhaps Oprah was simply tired of it all.

Yet shortly after Franzen's sprawling 2001 novel *The Corrections* was selected as a member of her club, and he made remarks in public to the effect this would cheapen his book, Oprah was finished with literary authors.

Such a pity. Those authors were finally making some real money from the publicity of Oprah's warm and vast spotlight.

Franzen seemed not to suffer a bit, aside from a few angry denunciations of him as an "elitist." Despite the lofty insults, critics and readers agreed the guy really could write. His novel topped the best-seller charts and won the National Book Award – an honor he was careful not to disparage.

Whenever a writer succeeds with a "breakthrough" novel, publishers are eager to follow up with ... something. The problem is literary authors tend not to be on the production treadmill of a John Grisham or Sue Grafton, who seem able to spill a novel off their personal assembly lines every year.

Certain writers require more time to dream and more seasons to ripen.

So, as filler and as a sop to their demanding yet possibly fickle readers, newly successful literary writers tend to clean out their files and put out collections of short stories and essays, almost all of which have appeared previously in various small magazines or university journals. Such collections are supposed to calm the appetites of the fans until the writer comes up with another meaty novel – the real deal – similar to the way a mother throws Cheerios on the tray of a squalling toddler as she runs around the kitchen, frantically preparing the real meal.

Thus we have Franzen's current offering, *How to Be Alone: Essays*, consisting of 13 journalism pieces covering a range of subjects from his father's Alzheimer's disease to the Chicago Post Office to prisons to the state of literary fiction in America.

The collection, including a few stale Cheerios, presents itself in no chronological or thematic order. In a useful introduction, Franzen tells us he intends this book "as a record of a movement away from an angry and frightened isolation toward an acceptance – even a celebration – of being a reader and a writer."

Okay, we can all use more of that. He also wants to take a crack at "the problems of preserving individuality and complexity in a noisy and distracting mass culture: the question of how to be alone."

I like Franzen. I liked his brassy denunciation of a dubious honor and I liked his big novel and the fact it was a huge success. He's tortured and funny and angry (still) and incredulous.

You kind of wonder where it all comes from, however, as he recounts his fairly normal, happy Midwestern boyhood, guarded by affectionate parents and marred only by typical adolescent embarrassments. He possesses not only a retentive memory for everything he has seen, heard, smelled or read, but also humor and a killer vocabulary.

Ten of his essays are worth reading, but three should have been discarded. For this sort of book, that is a fine ratio. Franzen's secret is speaking truth.

He speaks, for instance, about privacy and how as a country we worry we are being watched and invaded and we have nowhere to hide. Franzen turns this around, making the common sense observation that we are isolated emotionally with too little genuine interaction. We must listen constantly to the cell phone conversations of strangers. We are flooded with information about the sexual indiscretions of public figures.

Yet such information is meaningless to us personally. Television has made so many intimate subjects a part of public discourse there is little shame. Nothing is taboo. "Privacy," Franzen tells us, "loses its value unless there's something it can be defined against."

Interesting to encounter someone who thinks if we threw out our TV sets we might read more Henry James and be better off for it, who despairs over the apparent death of the social novel yet offers us the unsentimental observation, a "simple truth, if unpretty. The novel is dying because the consumer doesn't want it anymore."

If true, how devastating to conclude your chosen life's work, your passion is dismissed by the people you must reach. No wonder Franzen is, as he admits, frequently depressed. Thank goodness he soldiers on, holding together that small community of readers and writers who are trying to "preserve a tradition of precise, expressive language, a habit of looking past surfaces into interiors."

Thank goodness Franzen is humble enough to want his work to be "enjoyed, not taken as medicine." In the most forthright statement I've read on the subject, he declares, "Ultimately, if novelists want their work to be read, the responsibility for making it attractive and imperative is solely their own."

Yes! No more blaming the fact that people do not read on the culture, television, drugs, or the distractions of mass materialism and shopping. No more expecting Oprah to select books and spoon-feed them to us. If novelists want readers to be transformed and rescued (Franzen's word) by literature, they must make it indispensable.

Does the author achieve his purpose? Does he instruct us on how to be alone? Not quite, though he makes it pleasant to be alone with him for a while. His unique voice, conversational and alert, draws us close.

While reading *How to Be Alone*, I imagined an unusual friend from the past had called and talked on and on, catching up on a lifetime of thought and experience. Even after hours and hours, I was thinking: "Don't hang up. Keep going."

(*How to Be Alone: Essays* by Jonathan Franzen. Farrar, Strauss and Giroux, 2002. 278 pages)

A divine 'Emperor'
January 28, 2003

In an odd juxtaposition of history repeating itself, I saw a photograph in The Washington Post of Arab men lining up to be registered and questioned on the very day I finished reading a current novel about Japanese internment during World War II.

The fear and uncertainty showing in the men's faces and their hunched shoulders contrasted with their stylish Western clothing and generally prosperous appearance. The picture echoed the opening theme of Julie Otsuka's shimmering novella *When the Emperor Was Divine*.

The story begins a few days after Pearl Harbor. In California, a man is arrested and taken from his comfortable home at night in his robe and slippers. Later, his wife reads on a billboard: "Evacuation Order No. 19." She begins to prepare her children for compliance with this order, packing suitcases with necessities for a trip to a destination unknown to them. Within the first dozen pages, the mother performs an execution both loving and violent, a deed she is still free to choose in a world that will soon give her no choice.

The drama in *Emperor* is played out in three spare acts, the first detailing how the mother and her children are transported to Utah where they are housed in desert barracks. The second portrays the ordeal of internment itself and the third renders the stark return home.

Otsuka perfectly describes the loneliness of separation and strangeness of odors and sounds in unfamiliar places. She never names her fictional family, only tells us the father is 52, the mother 41 and the daughter and son ages 10 and 7. During the four years of exile, the children communicate with their father by sending postcards and occasional letters to his place of incarceration in New Mexico.

The central experience of the exile is given to us through the boy's impressions and observations of those around him. Dreams figure prominently as a means of mental escape or passing tedious hours of confinement. He dreams of wild mustangs and of his father, the father who provided well for his family, who loved to joke and sing, who wore elegant shoes and a rakish hat. The boy remembers their life together on "the tree-lined streets at sundown, the dark green lawns, boys throwing balls in backyards, mothers ... sliding hot casseroles out of ovens, fathers with shiny briefcases bursting through front doors, shouting 'Honey, I'm home!' Dinnertime across America."

It is a marvelous, idyllic America they have lived in. Yet when the war comes, they are singled out as different from the "real" Americans. It is a matter of "national security," they are told, an "opportunity to prove their loyalty."

The more things change, the more they remain the same.

Although the mother burns family photographs and silk kimonos and records of Japanese opera and smashes Imari dishes and the abacus, telling her children to count on their fingers, and though she ceases to send rice balls to school in the lunch pails, sending instead peanut butter and jelly – still the family must go. The parents have lived in America for 20 years but even so they are suspect.

It hurts to read certain cold facts. When asked, as they frequently are, whether they are Chinese or Japanese, the children are taught to answer, "Chinese." By denying their ethnic heritage, the mother is only trying to protect them.

Has anything changed? Are we still making rude and bumbling mistakes, lumping together people of various Middle-Eastern nationalities and acting suspicious of everyone, causing fear among innocents?

Although there is no talk at present of interning Arab-Americans while we fight this war on terror, the parallels are obvious and thought-provoking.

Who is ultimately to blame for brokenness that cannot be mended? The father is reunited with his family but never recovers from being stripped of his hat and shoes, his dignity. The mother manages to prevail. In a powerful coda, Otsuka compacts the entire broad experience into a deeply felt "Confession" that is unlike anything I've ever read, a passage that left me gasping in tears of admiration.

Otsuka based this story on some of her own family's personal history. Her grandfather was arrested and her grandmother was sent to a camp with Otsuka's mother and uncle. Because her relatives never reminisced about the war and even refused to teach their children Japanese, the author had to research the internment experience and imagine what it was like. Her novel somewhat evokes Anne Frank's diary and the recent *Snow Falling on Cedars*, yet is not imitative in any way.

This slim volume possesses a unique voice, truly the author's own. Every scene, every moment is carved with precision. It is an exquisite novel, in the sense that a tastefully small diamond, brilliantly faceted, is polished to a solid, sparkling essence.

Consider this image: It is Christmas Day, bleak and bitter cold. The boy receives a small red Swiss Army knife from a Quaker organization's distribution of gifts. He promptly writes a thank you to the donor, a lady from Ohio. As he runs over a gray desert, the knife clacks against a lucky blue stone in his pocket and makes him feel temporarily very happy.

"His pockets were filled with good things," Otsuka tells us. Her prose in this lovely and wrenching novel spills over with many good things.

(*When the Emperor Was Divine* by Julie Otsuka. Knopf, 2002. 144 pages)

A gripping 'Panda' chase
February 8, 2003

The first panda brought out of China to survive in captivity was a baby named Su Lin – "a little bit of something cute." The name aptly sums up how the world has treated these exotic animals ever since – as adorable, fascinating, cuddly creatures. Crowds at zoos demonstrate we cannot get enough of them, of their rotund bodies and sweet faces and their plaintive-seeming, darkly masked eyes.

The capture of Su Lin is the central story in Michael Kiefer's *Chasing the Panda*, a truly rollicking tale of adventure, romance, jealousy and mystery that recounts the days of Great White Hunters in the first half of the 20th century.

This was an era of collecting mania to fill museums and populate zoos with attractions that drew paying customers from a growing leisure class, many of which joined in explorations to wild, untracked places.

Two such men were Ted and Kermit Roosevelt, sons of President Theodore. Bitten with the bug of wanderlust from accompanying their father on expeditions, they mounted several of their own. In the late 1920s, they prowled wild areas of China, seeking a strange white bear.

Enter another pair of brothers: Jack and Quentin Young. The two men were Chinese but born in America. They spoke several languages and dialects and moved easily among countries and cultures. Jack, the elder, was smart and dashing and successful at almost anything he attempted. The younger Quentin, although tall and handsome, was shy and less self-assured.

The Roosevelts hired Jack to accompany them on their 1929 trek in search of panda. They actually managed to reach the elusive bamboo forest habitat of the panda. They shot a large specimen and returned the skin to the Field Museum in Chicago for stuffing. It was, as Keifer notes, as though they had brought back a unicorn, so great was the public's wonder at this alluring beast.

Then the race was on. Collectors everywhere clamored for the hide of these animals. Another "explorer" arrived on the scene: William H. Harkness, a moderately and idly wealthy gentleman with a yearning for adventure.

Along with a couple of friends, Harkness gained attention in the narrow field of international hunting and gathering when they captured 13 Komodo lizards – all over seven feet long – and brought them into captivity. These tricky and dangerous reptiles repeatedly flung themselves against the cages, "trying to get at the humans" beyond the bars. Still, Harkness wrestled three of them to American zoos, earning himself a heroic reputation and, more important, the ability to raise money for another expedition, this time for panda.

Harkness, after purchasing supplies and assembling a crew, died in Shanghai. His widow, Ruth, a fashion designer in New York, made her way to China to pick up the threads of William's quest. Ruth Harkness quickly becomes the heroine of this story.

At 35, she made a shrewd decision to hire Jack Young's 22-year old brother Quentin to lead her into the wild hinterland in a search to capture – not kill – a panda. Ruth's sheer determination impressed her untested guide, and his good looks and daring certainly made an impression on her. They became "involved," in the modern vernacular, yet did not lose sight of the main event.

Somewhere on the Sichuan-Tibetan border, 2,000 miles from their departure point of Shanghai, on the snowy morning of November 19, 1936, Quentin Young pulled a baby panda from a tree trunk and handed it to Ruth Harkness, who raced back to camp to begin feeding the infant from a bottle. She named the cub Su Lin. Carrying him for weeks in a backpack, Ruth eventually got through all the regulatory red tape and delivered him to the Brookfield Zoo outside Chicago.

Of course, there is much more to the story, most of it quite exciting and some of it a little sad.

Ruth returned to find a mate for her panda, dodging the opposing forces of Chinese civil war and also the Japanese, who by that time had invaded the mainland.

Among the community of hunters, rivalries broke out from the heat of publicity and money. China was pillaged of its treasure at an alarming rate. The rapacious frenzy to seize these animals led to random slaughter until the Chinese government shut down all operations in 1939.

It is gripping to read about this period of history, to imagine climbing narrow treacherous paths to high snow-covered lamaseries in the clouds, to drink yak butter tea with tribal princesses and casually eat white pheasant worth thousands to curators around the civilized world.

Although the lure of this interesting material is superior to Keifer's skill as a writer, he handles his large cast of colorful characters well. Wonderful vintage photographs accompany the text and help the narrative to come alive. I wished for maps also and had to make do with running to my own atlas.

While reading several passages, I thought: Wow, what a great movie this would be! Near the end, Keifer reveals that indeed, in the late 1990s, a film was made of this remarkable true story. Yet in a frustrating omission, he does not give the title. (So I will give it. It was made in the giant IMAX format and is called "China: The Panda Adventure.")

Keifer's writing of this book evolved over a decade of research and interviews with the principals or surviving relatives. After many years of intrigue and various successes and failures, the Young brothers retired in America. They generously gave the author old letters and articles and, in addition, befriended him. At this writing, Quentin remains alive and living near St. Louis.

Su Lin was not so fortunate. He died of pneumonia at age 2, having grown to 225 pounds. His remains can be seen today at the Field Museum in an elegant glass case – along with a looped tape showing him romping playfully in his prime – and also on the jacket of this book, peeking from behind the shoulder of the author. A nice touch.

(*Chasing the Panda: How an Unlikely Pair of Adventurers Won the Race to Capture the Mythical 'White Bear'* by Michael Kiefer. Four Walls Eight Windows, 2002. 230 pages)

'Leonardo' meets computer
February 15, 2003

In one of life's little ironies, the very week I began reading *Leonardo's Laptop* – an absorbing book about new computing technologies – the modem for my MAC went haywire, and I spent days fuming and waiting for a fix. Professor Ben Shneiderman managed to hold my attention during that period with his insightful views and forward thinking on the subject of computers.

It is frustrating in the extreme to have computer problems. Once we become accustomed to a new and convenient technology, we tend to take it for granted and almost forget how to function otherwise.

I blush to confess how annoyed I was recently when driving a rental car without automatic windows or remote-key entry. There are other examples of this sort too trivial to mention. Yet I am unembarrassed to say I just hate it when my computer is down. I want to turn it on the way I do my dishwasher and see it work through the cycle.

Which is why Shneiderman's book was so comforting. He understands this trauma completely and is convinced this must be the focus of future computer technology – reducing frustration for the user while at the same time enhancing delight in these machines.

Shneiderman begins with this premise: Computers to date have put technology first. He calls this "old computing." In the wonderful world of "new computing," we will see a much more user-friendly era – the users being you and me.

Meanwhile, he outlines many present problems of poorly designed software, wasted hours of crashes and downtime and failures of all types. He acknowledges the anger people experience when attempting to install balky upgrades and the fear of losing files in transition. He quotes historian Lewis Mumford, who stated the goal of technology must be to "serve human needs." What humble brilliance!

Shneiderman explains how difficult this might be to achieve. Computer scientists and IT professionals are highly introverted people who would rather work in isolation than suffer the discomforts in dealing with the problems of actual users, he says. They are more interested in pure technology – what the computer can do – than what the user might need to do.

The professor likens shifting this point of view to the difficulties of Copernicus and Galileo endured persuading scholars the sun was at the center of the universe.

Throughout his book, the author uses Leonardo da Vinci and reproductions of his works as an "inspirational muse" to lead us into brave and futuristic thinking – an excellent choice. The original Renaissance man, an icon for the ages, used his inquisitive and independent mind to create powerful works of creative genius and established a rich legacy in art and science.

A few years ago, Bill Gates purchased Leonardo's notebooks for around 30 million dollars. These "notebooks" consisted of loose papers covered with cramped, almost unreadable scribbles.

Evidently, as Leonardo moved from palaces to artists' studios or along the streets and markets, several notebooks always dangled from his belt. He used them to jot down ideas and sketches and, thankfully, most of these works are easily decipherable. He left behind engineering plans for machines and drawings of statues impossible to build in his lifetime because the technologies had not been invented. He could only dream and design in ways that one day might have application.

Shneiderman imagines a modern Leonardo II with many Web sites and wall-sized projections. The figure presented here of the great Leonardo, busily trying to integrate art and science in the service of practical purpose and human needs, is delightful.

In the same vein, Shneiderman offers visions of future human-computer interaction (HCI) and interface designs that will be useful and enjoyable and even improve one's ability to expand relationships with family, friends and co-workers.

I love his concept of the InfoDoor. It is a Palm Pilot display with an Internet connection placed on office doors. A visitor or colleague could leave a message, learn your whereabouts, offer suggestions or any number of useful bits of communication.

The point is we are in an evolutionary pattern with computers. As with automobiles, we will move away from production-controlled products into considering what the consumer wants and demands. Just as we grew to want safer and more comfortable cars, it seems we now desire less complicated software, faster ways to keep in touch with people and easier access to information.

Shneiderman considers how new computing could apply to many broad social issues, such as more equitable use among various economic and age levels and greater empowerment in learning, healthcare, business and government.

Whether or not you agree with his theories and enter into his imaginative scenarios, this able professor challenges you to think about the ways we receive and use information and disseminate this into ideas or art.

I think sitting in his classroom might be fun and enlightening. He is blessed with an engaging writing style and the ability to make this material interesting and lively. Even more, he presents a reader with possibilities and hope. What a wonderful accomplishment.

(*Leonardo's Laptop: Human Needs and the New Computing Technologies* by Ben Shneiderman. The MIT Press, 2003. 281 pages)

Pearls among 'Pinstripes'
March 1, 2003

Dressed for success in the power suit of dominant males yet adding her mother's necklace for luck, Judith Richards Hope stormed barricades of gender prejudice in the practice of law and broke trails for generations of women who followed.

Her career seems to be one of steadily climbing a ladder of rungs marked "First" – first woman to sit on certain corporate boards, first woman named to Harvard's governing board, first female associate director of the White House Domestic Council. This is one impressive lady.

"Lady" is an important word in her vocabulary. In *Pinstripes & Pearls*, as she chronicles her class of Harvard Law School '64, in which Hope is one of 15 women in a field of 513 graduates, she makes the case that ladylike behavior and dress were the preferred norm.

These bright, ambitious women wore skirts and heels to lectures and accepted inferior status in substandard housing and campus restroom facilities. The women formed important connections to sustain one another and took pride in not complaining. Determined to have it all – distinguished careers and fulfilling marriages – rather than trying to change the status quo, they took it in stride, becoming what Hope labels the "suck it up" generation. They never showed pain at insults or admitted to fatigue or, most important, quit.

Harvard Law School. The words alone are intimidating, connoting academic excellence achieved through brutal schedules and fierce competition. Legions of graduates testify to its life-defining experience leading to prosperous, distinguished careers ... if it doesn't kill you.

Stories of first-year Harvard Law intensity have been told previously and thoroughly by Scott Turow in *One L* and John J. Osborn Jr. in *The Paper Chase*. What Hope adds to the mix is the sharp observance of humiliation and exhilaration from her woman's point of view and that of her classmates.

"The sound I remember most from classes is laughter," she writes.

Hope calls her class "legendary," which does not appear to be a stretch. Among others it produced Congresswoman Pat Schroeder, Judge Judith Rogers of the U.S. Court of Appeals and many professors, partners of law firms and high government officials.

Janet Reno, the former attorney general, graduated just one year ahead, and Elizabeth Dole, now senator from North Carolina, followed one year behind. The male members are equally imposing, including Stephen G. Breyer, associate justice of the U.S. Supreme Court.

One does not quarrel with the fact this talented bunch of women worked hard and earned their success.

Hope recounts fascinating details of the difficulties many faced, even after receiving their degrees. The big law firms simply did not hire women, no matter what their grades and credentials were. The thinking was a married woman was sure to have a baby or did not really need a job because she had a husband to support her. If single, she surely would marry soon and have a baby. Such attitudes and practices were hard to crack. For most of the women, it was a matter of finding a side entrance or a slightly opened window to slide through.

In writing this history, Hope gives us facts about the slow acceptance of women into the upper reaches of academe along with the pitiful statistics of how few women actually practiced law well into the 20th century.

Unfortunately, her attempts to describe the popular culture of the times – TV shows, activities, political movements – are not well done and come across as stilted. Perhaps she was too busy studying to get into all that stuff. The most glaring omission is her failure to document what it was like to experience the day of John Kennedy's assassination on the Harvard campus – his alma mater. Surely that was a devastating and altering event, and what a missed opportunity to provide an eyewitness account.

Much of Hope's book is written in the form of lengthy yearbook-type entries about her classmates and how they are doing. Only occasionally does she drift into the area of braggy, alumni-newsletter updates. I really enjoyed the portraits – snapshots, really – of these bright and breezy girls forging into life and jobs and relationships without always knowing how it would all turn out. Her generation did not expect guarantees.

As I read along, I found myself casting the movie: Pat Schroeder, a pilot in her teens, earning her way through college and driving to Harvard in a turquoise Continental bought with her own money, suggests a young Katharine Hepburn. Ann Dudley, with her mini-skirts, flashy figure and sassy intellect, seems perfect for Reese Witherspoon. And for Judith Hope herself, who else but Joanne Woodward with her calm and correct exterior but projecting plenty of firepower underneath?

Entertaining thoughts all, and although I found the book informative and fun to read – despite my wanting to wince at the affronts the women suffered – why, at the end, did I feel, a bit cheated?

I think it's because of the odd narrative technique Hope employs, the frequent use of the collective "we," as in, "We were out of the ordinary," or, "Most of us were first-born or only children," or "in our mind's eyes."

It becomes disconcerting to read "we thought" and "we liked to flirt," as though the women were one giant moving body and mind instead of interesting and distinct individuals. Hope seems to have chosen this style as a sort of protective cover because although she reveals delicious details about her classmates in the biographical sketches – including sexual intimacies – she is reticent about her own emotions.

Too often, Hope distances herself from the reader just when I wished she would zero in on her personal life and choices. Her marriage to the son of entertainer Bob Hope seems to flit across a few pages and be gone, while her interview and tutelage with super lawyer Edward Bennett Williams is meaty and deep.

He told her something quite memorable before hiring her at age 24: "A woman has the edge. Your job is to figure out how to use it." I assume she did just that.

Hope would not have achieved her status without smarts, drive and, frankly, guts. Perhaps her gutsiest choice in composing the book was to include written report cards from her children.

Her son Zachary is fairly admiring and kind, but daughter Miranda obviously has "issues." What mother would not cringe hearing herself described as too invincible, too pushy, too isolated, too sedentary, too tired?

"A woman I have never seen truly laugh or truly cry," Miranda also discloses. "A woman without needs. A tank." This is all said with love, of course, and I admire Judith Hope most for allowing that image of her to seep in after the litany of constant triumphs.

It's probably not fair to compare *Pinstripes & Pearls* to Katherine Graham's *Personal History*, the extraordinarily honest, elegant, woman-in-a-man's-profession book published a few years back. But this one, even with its awkward style, delivers a punch in describing what seems like ancient history on the timeline of women's progress toward equality with men.

Are we there yet?

(*Pinstripes & Pearls: The Women of the Harvard Law Class of '64 Who Forged an Old-Girl Network and Paved the Way for Future Generations* by Judith Richards Hope. Simon & Schuster, 2003. 320 pages)

'Food' for thought
March 6, 2003

A few years ago, I read a book of superior advice to writers by Betsy Lerner, a former editor at Simon & Schuster. The author was unknown to me, but her voice on the page flowed with such warmth, intelligence, humor and encouragement I immediately thought I'd found a new friend. She seemed especially perceptive about the rough patches in a writer's process.

So when I spied Lerner's name on a new book, I grabbed it without hesitation. Her latest work, *Food and Loathing*, recounts her battles with undiagnosed manic depression and overeating from childhood to the present.

I read it the way she describes scarfing down Krispy Kremes – I could not stop turning pages.

I felt guilty, in a way. From her earlier work, I assumed I "knew" her – a smart, witty lady who knew her way around the publishing business. Having all the details filled in was kind of delicious and scary at the same time – much like the way she reveals the allure of her secret feedings.

In her first book, Lerner repeats a statement J. D. Salinger made to his young protégé and lover Joyce Maynard: "Honest writing always makes people nervous."

I kept thinking of that wonderful quote as I read *Food and Loathing*. I salute the astonishing honesty of this memoir even though it caused me to squirm. The author stares down the reader with her unblinking, relentless truth. Nothing bashful about this story. Do not expect triumphs or coyly flattering vignettes. She includes no pity-me passages and blames no one.

Lerner grew up in a comfortable suburb of New Haven. By the age of 12, she finds herself dreading the public embarrassment of gym-class weigh-ins in the presence of skinny friends. Ah, the good old days before the self-esteem police entered the educational system and declared keeping score in games and even choosing valedictorians damaged the fragile psyches of our young with unfair comparisons.

Escapism from that earlier sweaty torture comes for Lerner in attending movies with her adored father and sharing sweet snacks. Her mother's attempts to be helpful in selecting a slimming wardrobe cause nothing but more adolescent agony.

At 15, Lerner joins Overeaters Anonymous, then a barely formed organization based on a 12-step program of abstention.

She takes this on like a religion and – miracle of miracles – loses 50 pounds and attracts a bona fide boyfriend for the first time.

If only her story could end on this Cinderella note!

Real life has a way of frustrating happy endings. Who would think of an Eskimo Pie as lethal? Lerner gains it all back and enters a period of grappling with other problems. Her weight bounces up and down, as do her emotions. An earlier death of a younger sister haunts her through recurring dreams of a sinister wolf. Even with two sisters living, she cannot understand how little girls just get eaten up. Depression sinks her buoyant spirit, assisted by a therapist so incompetent I hope Lerner has used his real name as a warning to unsuspecting others.

She self-medicates her self-loathing with reckless substance abuse, making her appearance as unattractive as possible, casual sex and, of course, food. All she wants is to learn how to cope, somehow, with her inner turmoil and rampant appetites. Her peculiar curse is being able to fake it so well for so long. Yet even as she attends college, wins a prize for her poetry and holds down a credible job, she spirals out of control and lands in a psych ward in New York after a suicidal episode.

Lerner writes about terrible personal moments without losing her grip and sliding into despair. You never forget this is a bright and funny young woman engaged in a monumental struggle. I started rooting for her right around page 3.

How lovely to learn she marries a great guy and has a daughter and a fulfilling career. But it's not a perfect ending. She still fights the scale, worries about her child becoming obese and earns her happiness day to day.

Lerner does not exactly offer any new revelations here. Feeling bad about oneself can arise from many sources, and self-destruction can take many forms. Getting well is ever hard work.

Yet Lerner offers her own unique version of these realities, and I'd rather have that than a dozen Oreos.

(*Food and Loathing: A Lament* by Betsy Lerner. Simon & Schuster, 2003. 304 pages)

'Extremely Happy' company
March 20, 2003

Has there been a more inspired pairing in the history of exploration than Meriwether Lewis and William Clark? Will our appetite for tales of these men seeking a Northwest passage through uncharted territory ever be satisfied?

As the bicentenary of their daring adventure approaches, Brian Hall offers a fresh vision of the Corps of Discovery, more commonly known as the Lewis and Clark expedition, in a novel called *I Should Be Extremely Happy in Your Company*. Hall shapes his fictional account using excerpts from letters, diaries and the famous journals yet invents conversations and creates portraits of characters based on sometimes limited recorded evidence.

At first, I questioned the need for such a work. After all, has biography exhausted itself? As a teenager, I stumbled by chance onto the Bernard DeVoto edition of the *Journals of Lewis and Clark* and just fell in love with true stories of heroic high adventure. I've remained devoted to this infatuation. I adore Lewis and Clark and was somewhat annoyed that anyone would try to fabricate scenes of such an historic quest.

Yet I must say, very quickly, the narrative caught me as though in a river's current and carried me along. The research is careful, respectful and – may I say? – loving. Hall's original insights allow one to enjoy a remarkable achievement all over again.

He begins with Lewis living in the White House, serving as personal secretary to President Jefferson and performing all sorts of tasks from shooting game to copying letters to simply dining with "Mr. J's pale eyes." Lewis bunks and dreams in a canvas tent pitched in the East Room. Mr. J busily notes the weather each day in his journal and keeps track of each seed germinated at his beloved estate, Monticello. Together, in a rarified atmosphere, they plan the mission.

The first brilliant decision enlists William Clark, an Army lieutenant Lewis met on campaigns in Pennsylvania.

"Pound the two men and cook them in a crucible, and pour out William Meriwether Lewis Clark," writes Hall.

I'm not sure I agree with that, equal though they were in leadership, Lewis insisting on both being "captains." Actually, Hall does a fine job of differentiating the men's personalities. Lewis, or "Big Knife" as the Indians called him, is handsome, educated, accustomed to exercising authority and skilled in frontier survival. Clark, or "Red Hair," has proven himself capable in military service and has definitely won the complete confidence and admiration of Lewis.

Hall imagines Lewis fretting over whether Clark is the better man, with greater endurance, more natural qualities. He even wonders, as he scribbles in the journals, making endless notes for Mr. J., if Clark is not a better writer, more original, less encumbered by attempting stylistic flourishes. Intrepid Clark, unbothered by such musings, worries only occasionally about a number of fair ladies back home.

It's fascinating to see how Hall embellishes familiar events set down in the journals. The long days of man-hauling heavy boats to gain perhaps a mile or two, the men inching forward on "torn and bleeding feet." The agonizing birth of Sacagawea's little boy.

A day when the journals washed overboard and were almost lost in the raging river. The first sighting of a grizzly bear.

A thrilling chapter describes the time Lewis goes in advance of the party to search for food and shoots a buffalo. Before reloading, he is confronted by a huge bear and must run for his life. Completely alone in the wilderness, he does not lose a drop of nerve. His men, out searching for him, at last call out, "God have mercy, Captain! Are you all right?" And Lewis answers, "Never mind that!" A singing in his ears. Jubilation. "What's for supper?"

Hall renders the speech patterns of the characters and the inner thoughts of Lewis with ringing authenticity and brilliant pre-Freudian perception. His command of language lifts understanding of this well-known story to a new level. Perhaps his most audacious yet delightful inventions are those of Clark's faithful black servant York and the Shoshone teenage guide Sacagawea. York becomes the equal of any man on the expedition, a real presence, and the young woman comes alive through a unique voice Hall devises. A scene in which she names herself is sheer poetry.

The author carries his narrative beyond the triumphal return to St. Louis and splitting up of the happy "band of brothers," revealing what happens to the main characters and even "solving" the mystery of Lewis's ambiguous death. Interesting stuff all the way and very satisfying. I was completely won over by this writer and found his to be an exceptional variant of a thrilling American saga. Hall selected material that was pure gold to begin with and gave it even more glimmer and sheen. A rarity, I think, in historical literary fiction.

(*I Should Be Extremely Happy In Your Company: A Novel of Lewis and Clark* by Brian Hall. Viking Adult, 2003. 432 pages)

'Book Club' a must-read
March 27, 2003

During times of stress, a most welcome gift is a book so absorbing it helps to focus the mind and provide respite from troubled reality. Paula Huntley's *The Hemingway Book Club of Kosovo* is such a book.

I ran across this volume during a quick breeze-through of my local library, where the title leaped out at me. What a lucky find it proved to be.

The work is about war, tyranny, atrocities, poverty, endless struggle and hopelessness. Yet it gave my spirit a real lift because it also is about tolerance, respect for others, patience and love.

Its premise is simple. In the spring of 2000, Huntley's husband, Ed Villmoare, proposes that he take a leave of absence from teaching law and the two of them go to Kosovo for a year. He hopes to work at creating a legal system in the formerly Yugoslav province, now "the first country to be completely administered by the United Nations."

Freely admitting she knows little about Kosovo but energetically curious, Huntley goes along with the plan, demonstrating, I would say, at the very least she is a darn good sport.

From the moment she steps off the plane in the capital city of Prishtina, her narrative draws one into a world of messy half-built structures, of streets and sidewalks piled deeply with trash, of the stench of rotting food permeating the dangerously polluted air. A city, she tells us, where "nothing looked quite plumb."

After settling into an exorbitantly expensive rental house – all the "internationals" flooding into town have driven prices sky-high – Huntley casts about for some useful way to spend her time while Ed is working. Her career skills in marketing are not in demand in Prishtina; there is nothing to sell in this poor city. An opportunity presents itself to teach English at the Cambridge School, an enterprise set up in a former sports complex, now almost in ruins.

Huntley jumps at the chance and changes her life forever. When she enters this scene, the Kosovo Albanians are about a year past the liberating war from persecution by the Serbs. The situation is still very tenuous and scary at times. KFOR troops – the U.N.-NATO forces – are present everywhere. After many years of apartheid and repression, of being killed or driven from their homes and returning to find them burned, these Albanians are loving their freedom, loving the Americans who made it possible but not wanting any other ethnic group to reside in their newly democratic country.

Huntley, writing in journal form, does as good a job as I've read anywhere explaining what's going on in the Balkans. This complicated political and cultural environment usually defeats my understanding. I am grateful for her primer, for the way she brings it home and makes this subject somehow intelligible.

At the heart of this story is Huntley's love affair with her students, beautiful young people, bright and enthusiastic, who both laugh and work hard. Yet she sees "behind each eager smiling face ... a hidden memory of grief, terror, loss. Everyone here has been wounded."

The class meets around a large table, working with tattered texts and inadequate supplies. Ages range from young teens to some graduate students in their twenties. The common bond is their ardent desire to learn English – seen as the key to advancement and success – and the ability to pay tuition of $25 a month. This fee is a huge consideration in a country where the average family earns "only enough to buy food for one week each month."

Huntley, although not a teacher by profession, in nonetheless competent and caring, a natural. Feeling overwhelmed at her students' dependence on her, finding their faith in her "frightening" at times, she more than rises to the challenge with innovative methods. Searching about for a book they can all read together, she finds a paperback of Hemingway's *The Old Man and the Sea* and makes copies for everyone.

"You give us books. No one else does this for us ever," says Leonard, her most serious student.

The "book club" meets at "dear teacher's" house. Huntley sketches pictures of difficult words like "skiff" and "harpoon." As the class works through the story, relating to the old man and his tenacity in catching a fish, Huntley draws from them their own stories, of how they fled their homes, of what happened to their families before and during the war. They write heartrending compositions in fledgling English, not unlike the spare Hemingway style, telling what it is like to walk at last on the streets unafraid.

In describing her students, Huntley makes each one live and even sing on the page. By the end of the book, I wanted to adopt every one of them. And why not? They all want to come to America, to get good jobs and help their families.

"America is our dream," they tell her.

When Huntley returns to her comfortable home north of San Francisco overlooking the Pacific Ocean, she understandably enjoys breathing healthy air again and seeing the deep blue of the ocean. Yet she stays connected to her class in Kosovo and works to help them in countless ways. The country itself has seized some tender thread in her heart and it unspools in this book.

Huntley presents landscapes described as medieval or horrifying, layered with raw, modern, but crudely thrown-together buildings. Pristina sounds like some early American western boomtown, rather lawless and edgy. What must it be like to attend a Kosovo Philharmonic concert and afterward listen to guns firing all night?

These weird juxtapositions and the author's unvaryingly fascinating observations give this book a pulse. She solves no problems, nor claims to. In a tiny part of the world where there was only despair, the gains are minuscule and perishable. In some ways, Huntley leaves a reader with anxious questions. What she has accomplished is putting a face on a complex region and causing a reader to look at it with compelling interest.

Huntley is not a writer by trade, but in this work, she has written something very fine and, I think, lasting. You will not easily forget the members of this book club.

(*The Hemingway Book Club of Kosovo* by Paula Huntley. Jeremy P. Tarcher/Putnam, 2003. 236 pages)

Take the 'Power' trip
April 3, 2003

Anyone even slightly tuned in to world events of the past few months knows America and Europe are in a dysfunctional relationship. According to Robert Kagan in his new book, *Of Paradise and Power*, the present "transatlantic divide" might be headed for divorce court.

I read his book in one sitting for two reasons. First, Kagan is an excellent writer; observant and witty. An American, he has lived in Belgium for several years and has gained access and insight into the nuanced culture and attitudes of Europe.

Through his regular columns in The Washington Post, I became aware of the growing anti-Semitism and anti-Americanism openly expressed at the conferences and gatherings European intellectuals so love to attend.

The second reason I whipped through the volume is its slender size – barely 100 pages. If it were fiction, it would be a novella – or, perhaps, a "noveleeny." The brevity aside, Kagan says a lot in his trenchant, elegant sentences. He begins by blasting away the notion Americans and Europeans share similar views of the world. As he puts it, "the United States and Europe have parted ways."

Because of the terrible wars and uneasy peace arrangements of several centuries, Europeans attempt to solve problems through "subtlety and indirection." They prefer an endless process of negotiation, diplomacy, coercion and appeal to international law and conventions to reaching an actual resolution.

Americans, on the other hand, possess an amazing persistence in pushing for solutions to problems. We are not averse to using our various powers to force change if we see this as necessary to achieve a common good.

Kagan employs many apt examples to show the ways these differences play out on the world stage. He does not have to work too hard to persuade any reader who witnessed the recent futile struggles in the United Nations.

His book might serve as the script for a drama in which the actors played their parts to perfection. As Kagan sees it, there is a serious power gap between the two sides, along with a broad ideological gap, making it unlikely this divisive trend will be reversed.

Europeans genuinely fear another devastating war. They have worked to create their European Union, binding countries together in trade, currency and commonality, barricading themselves against the notion of going to war against one another ever again.

Therefore, they enjoy a sort of "perpetual peace." They extol their social programs and short workweeks and do not wish to bear the cost of maintaining military strength.

And why not? The United States for decades has done that for them, providing the deterrent to the threat of Soviet aggression. "American power," writes Kagan, "made it possible for Europeans to believe that power was no longer important."

In the post-Cold War world, Europe finds American military strength to be dangerous, so they disdain it and devalue it.

Kagan uses several sharp analogies to explain the situation. For instance, Europeans love to call Americans "cowboys." And Kagan likes this. The United States does act like an "international sheriff, self-appointed perhaps but widely welcomed nonetheless, trying to enforce some peace and justice ... often through the muzzle of a gun."

Europe, in this scenario, is the saloonkeeper. Outlaws seldom shoot saloonkeepers, only sheriffs. The saloonkeeper gets to duck behind the bar when the fighting starts.

Kagan seems comfortable with the notion of America's military power, calling us a "behemoth with a conscience." He persuaded me our founding fathers in fact intended America to be strong as a means of spreading our ideas and maintaining our freedom.

Although fond, I think, of European society in general, Kagan believes the new EU could easily spend the money necessary to put together a military force – not gargantuan, merely efficient. This would elevate their influence in the world, allow them to conduct diplomacy from a position of strength and, frankly, remove the embarrassment at such continued weakness.

Kagan writes he does not hold out hope for this, however. America will go forward, building our force, responding to "strategic challenges around the world" without much help from Europe – because we already do this.

Of Paradise and Power reads like a well-written term paper by the brightest guy in the class. I underlined and highlighted a lot because the text argues its points in perfect topic sentences, easy to follow and logically presented.

At times, Kagan assumes a reader understands issues about the Suez Canal or Hobbesian philosophy without much explication. But this is minor. One can always look it up.

Kagan's book could not be timelier. The author tackles a huge, obstinate subject, with complexities and potentially turgid contentions, and condenses his views into a serious yet pleasant read.

There's really no excuse for passing on this one. In the amount of time it takes to watch a bad movie, his book will leave one both entertained and enlightened.

(*Of Paradise and Power: America and Europe in the New World Order* by Robert Kagan. Knopf, 2003. 112 pages)

A well-rounded 'Crescent'
April 17, 2003

A thrilling achievement occurs in literary fiction when a writer manages to create a character so fascinating and memorable he "walks off the page" into reality. We all know such people: Scarlett O'Hara, Mr. Darcy, Heathcliff.

The hero of Diana Abu-Jaber's new novel, *Crescent*, could be one who steps into the consciousness of countless readers. He is Hanif Al Eyad, an intellectual, exotic linguist and translator of Poe, Whitman and even Hemingway into Arabic. His students at UCLA – male and female alike – sit bedazzled through his lectures and line up at his office for further instruction and conversation. As one of the besotted undergraduates explains: "Han teaches

Islamic history and Arabic literature, but he also teaches about life and art and faith and love – I mean if you know how to listen for it."

Listening happens to be a specialty of the beautiful Sirine, respected chef of surely the most appealing café in the "Irangeles" area near campus, part of the Westwood community populated with a mixture of Middle Eastern cultures. Having lost both parents at age 9, Sirine has been raised by her devoted uncle, another academic, living in a house filled with books and their "odor of forgotten memories." He tells Sirine a long involved story of a boy taken into slavery but escaping into many adventures and winding up with a true Hollywood ending.

The story spins on and on, snippets of which begin each chapter, full of fantasy and tragedy, humor and incredulous, constant events. It seems never to end. This tale provides a contrast to the greater narrative – the love story of Han and Sirine.

Uncle tells Sirine, "Stories are crescent moons; they glimmer in the night sky, but they are most exquisite in their incomplete state."

Incomplete would describe the community-seeking immigrant individuals Abu-Jaber gathers together in Nadia's café. Um-Nadia, the flamboyant Lebanese owner, presides over her customers as a mother hen, nudging the attraction between Sirine and Han into a romance.

How to explain the complexity of these people's lives? Han grew up in Iraq, a sleepier time, pre-Saddam. "In the Iraq of his childhood, everything went slowly. It took a lizard the entire course of the sun to walk from one side of his bedroom ceiling to the other." But events speeded up and Han left his native country for school in England and the opportunity to train his fine mind. He has not resolved the loneliness of his exile and remains haunted by what he left behind – his younger brother and sister in perilous situations.

Although half Iraqi herself, Sirine knows nothing of what Han suffers. Born in Los Angeles of an American mother, she only knows the Arab world through the filter of her uncle's stories. Yet embodied within her nature are both the Arab larger-than-life sense of "feelings walking in the sky" and a quieter patience, an ability to simply chop onions or stir a pot. Sirine believes "as long as she could cook, she would be loved."

Ah, but you must understand these two are gorgeous! Sirine's pale white blondeness, her hair so unruly it defies taming, attracts so many men she loses count. At 39, she remains unmarried and, even with her abundant lovers, sleeps in a chaste bed in her uncle's house.

Han is beautiful also, his voice "dark as chocolate with nuances of England and Eastern Europe, like a complicated sauce." When he and Sirine get together, images of food, music and fragrant breezes entangle in love scenes both timeless and of the moment. An interesting aspect of this story is the mature age of the principal characters, suggesting lives unfolding and taking shape before our eyes, a sort of ripening. Neither Han nor Sirine, although heavy with life experience, seems to have fully blossomed. As they wait and reveal the mysteries of themselves to each other, their futures hold many appetizing possibilities.

Abu-Jaber claims she began writing this novel years ago before Iraq drew the intense eyes of the world. Considering current events, her insights into Arab-American relations and various historical reflections naturally capture a reader's attention and, truthfully, I did soak up the passages pertaining especially to Iraq as a way to understand more about our charged international debate over a post-Saddam Middle East.

Yet putting that aside, *Crescent* does not need a context to qualify as an engaging read. If anything, it needs recipes of the fabulous dishes Sirine prepares! The author serves up her story as a fine meal of many courses to be enjoyed in leisurely fashion. The events presented here are not monumental – a poetry reading, a Thanksgiving dinner, a pool party or lunch at the café. But the backdrop is huge – families separated, individuals wrenched from their homelands, searching for connections and escaping cruel traditions. Although Abu-Jaber has put a lot on her plate, she blends the flavors and textures of her story with artistic integrity.

One of uncle's rules of storytelling is "You must never tell everything." I would say Abu-Jaber breaks that command. After stuffing the reader almost to the point of indigestion, of begging, please, no more, she offers a sweet dessert of an ending to complete her story.

I recommend this novel as I would a new restaurant. Go there, take your time and enjoy.

(*Crescent* by Diana Abu-Jaber. W.W. Norton & Company, 2003. 352 pages)

A 'Devil' with few details
April 24, 2003

I just finished reading *The Devil Wears Prada*, Lauren Weisberger's novel about the giddy and shallow but oh-so-fabulous world of Runway, a fictional New York fashion magazine. By "just finished," I mean I'm typing as fast as I can before the whole thing fades from my mind more quickly than froth on a cappuccino.

Qualifying by a mile for the role of "Devil" in the title is Miranda Priestly, editor in chief of Runway. Her world consists of clothes, nannies and chauffeurs, of serial husbands and bratty twin daughters, of underlings of all sorts who run about all day long trying to comply with her absurd, contradictory and utterly self-absorbed orders.

It is truly amazing so many otherwise sane-appearing people choose to work for this person – "the most powerful woman in fashion and publishing." The top excuse made for her behavior and ill-treatment of those around her is "you just can't get to the top of two major industries in New York City handing out candy all day long."

Definitely not receiving any candy is Andrea Sachs, fresh out of college and stumbling into the job as Miranda's assistant and gofer. People whisper over and over that her job is one "a million girls would kill for." Really? A million girls would debase themselves in the face of towering rudeness, low pay, chilly disdain and constant anger to sort their boss's dirty laundry?

I guess so, because the perks of working at Runway are stupendous – riding around Manhattan in chauffeured Lincoln Town Cars, expensing non-stop Starbucks lattes, and a gratis wardrobe of designer clothes, including handbags and shoes each costing enough to pay a year's rent. In one scene, Andrea handles a Dior dress for her boss carrying a price tag greater than the median family income in America.

Are the lowly indignities she suffers outweighed by the glamorous hobnobbing and glittering parties hosted by "the single most talented colorist in the civilized world"? That is the dilemma Andrea struggles with as she sees relationships with Alex, her decent teacher/boyfriend, and Lily, her troubled roommate, deteriorate while she submits more and more to Miranda's demands.

Andrea seems unable to escape Miranda's suffocating presence or her disembodied voice on the telephone. The constant, 24/7 ring of the cell phone causes Andrea to loathe "commercials for phones, pictures of phones in magazines and I even hated Alexander Graham Bell. Working for Miranda Priestly caused a number of unfortunate side effects in my day-to-day life, but the most unnatural one was my severe and all-consuming hatred of phones."

It becomes quickly apparent Andrea has no day-to-day life apart from cigarettes and caffeine. One must never eat in the presence of Miranda nor, really, while you're on duty at Runway, and that is all the time. The entire staff buys into the myth that one learns a lot from being around successful people, even though all one learns is to worship and slave. Our poor heroine loses weight, sleep and friends, all the while telling herself if she can just stick it out for a year, the experience and contacts will lead her to the job she really craves: writing for The New Yorker.

In the meantime, she tries to survive in this "different solar system," the world of fashion where the urgent need to get a certain skirt onto an airplane is difficult to translate in normal terms. It all seems to lack relevance.

One could say the same of this novel. I do not wish to be too harsh on a book meant to be pure escape, but it was difficult to sustain my interest. After Andrea lands the job, and after Miranda has whirled on and off the page a number of times, not much remains to keep it going. Fatigue sets in for the reader as well as for the characters, all of whom seem frantic and exhausted. The world of the rich and fashionable and hip just wears me out.

Reading about constant privileged waste is not amusing. A top New York chef, giggling with ecstasy, prepares a $95 lunch for Miranda, which she then blithely tosses in the garbage. Heels are wrenched off $800 shoes for no greater reason than Miranda's dog must go to the vet. To her credit, Weisberger does not allow Andrea to succumb to the lowest common denominator. She gets caught in the snare temporarily until her better nature takes over and all ends in an unobjectionable way.

The Devil Wears Prada reminds me somewhat of *The Nanny Diaries*, a best-seller a few seasons ago covering some of the same territory – the lives of the pampered and self-involved rich. It all wears thin after a short time. I found *Diaries* the more affecting read because of one character – the small neglected boy at the heart of the story. It helps to have someone to cheer for.

Unfortunately, it's difficult to care much about the people in Weisberger's novel. Miranda, in particular, never seems fleshed out. Rather, she's a composite of silly rich icons from the pages of Vanity Fair and Women's Wear Daily. Even Alex, Andrea's hapless boyfriend and an appealing guy, gets lost. The plot, such as it is, unfolds in endlessly repetitive scenes that provide a little juice for a moment and then dribble away.

Yet I would not count Weisberger out. This, her first novel, is not intellectual, wise or especially witty, but it is smart in a flashy way and occasionally funny. Odd, but I most enjoyed reading her acknowledgments – I found them original, humorous and confident. So perhaps better days are ahead for both author and heroine.

(*The Devil Wears Prada* by Lauren Weisberger. Doubleday, 2003. 360 pages)

No 'Shortcuts' indeed
May 2, 2003

A good teacher knows how to grab your attention and hold on to it. Rafe Esquith proves his skill in a memoir, *There Are No Shortcuts*, recounting 20 tumultuous years teaching fifth graders in an inner-city Los Angeles school he calls the Jungle.

Esquith begins his career at a dream school he dubs Camelot, where students come from affluent, literate families who are readily able to supplement classroom lessons with expensive field trips and extra-curricular materials. Initially delighted with his assignment to this "perfect school," Esquith is soon astonished to discover he feels unfulfilled and even physically ill with frustration.

Most of the students at Camelot cruise on autopilot toward assured, successful futures. Teachers are expected to go along with the status quo – even helping classes cheat in subtle ways on standardized tests in order to boost scores and receive more money for school programs.

Deeply troubled, knowing Camelot is wrong for him, Esquith makes a U-turn, taking a new job at a school he calls the Jungle. There, amid overcrowded classrooms where students test below grade level and most do not speak English at home, he finds rare happiness – but not right away.

A truly outstanding feature of this book is Esquith's honest description of his own learning curve. As a young teacher, inexperience and arrogance lead him to hurt, misery, even to failure. It is painful to read how desperately he struggles to make a difference in these children's lives. Driving himself mercilessly to be great, he seems to think of nothing but his work.

Part of his compulsion stems from a lack of proper role models. Sad, but neither of his parents lived to see him teach. Yet he absorbed a valuable lesson his father, a boxer: Always get up and answer the bell. A teacher is knocked down in many ways, but Esquith rises to the bell time and again.

Eventually, he finds inspiration to help him handle troubling situations with "grace, maturity and, most of all, results" in the figure of Atticus Finch from *To Kill a Mockingbird*. I like the way he analyzes fictional characters as learning tools. Especially fine is his explanation why Mr. Keating in the film "Dead Poets Society" is not a very good teacher.

Before he reaches this level of confidence, however, he makes many dubious choices. Determined to teach classics to 10-year-olds who have no money, he scrounges 36 copies of Steinbeck's *Of Mice and Men,* racing around to different libraries. He must dress in disguise to thwart the librarians' rules against checking out multiple copies of one title. He works two and three jobs in order to fund class trips, getting by with little sleep and ruining his health. He maxes out credit cards for the same reason, making a shambles of his finances.

Gradually, Esquith forms slightly more sensible habits, smiling at his noble excesses as "all heart and no brains." Yet part of his brain functions properly enough to formulate a work ethic allowing his students to thrive and astonish others with their intelligence, energy and creativity. Esquith believes these children are every bit as bright as those at Camelot, but they must work harder to overcome obstacles and achieve excellence.

Esquith has become well-known in educational circles, receiving countless awards and accolades for outstanding teaching methods that produce actual, measurable results – fifth graders who put on entire Shakespeare plays, who read (and comprehend) Arthur Miller's "The Crucible," who test well and go on to the top universities. To floundering educators teaching at this low socio-economic level, Esquith's accomplishments must seem like miracles.

This personal story testifies against miracles. Esquith's principles and methods are actually quite simple on the surface. He sets the bar high, arriving early and staying late, as do his pupils. He infuses them with a love of his favorite writers – Dickens, Twain, Shakespeare, of course – and helps them understand just why the works are great. He believes reading is the most important subject in school, period, and therefore extends his school day to make certain enough hours are devoted to it. He battles any hindrance to his students' progress with dogged zeal.

Naturally, this does not sit well at times with administrators and faculty. Perhaps Esquith is difficult in person. At times, passionate people can seem a bit insufferable and uncompromising. He says plenty about people in authority "who could not teach a group of students on their best day," repeating several times how easy it is to become angry. Yet he plugs away, year after year, at his vision of excellence, of students performing exciting concerts and plays, of winning math competitions, of traveling to foreign countries and dazzling spectators with their talent and exemplary manners.

To that end, he places two posters in his classroom: "There are no shortcuts" and "Be nice, work hard." Esquith's goals include developing not only superior academics but also wonderful human beings.

Frankly, I find it remarkable this man has remained, as he says, "a regular classroom teacher," not moving up into administration but sticking with his fifth graders and showing up every day at 6:30 a.m.

After reading this story, I felt deprived of a rich educational experience. I never had such a teacher but am grateful to meet one through this glowing work, filled with telling incidents and lively vignettes, heavy with life and possibility.

Homework for this weekend: Read *There Are No Shortcuts*. Class dismissed.

(*There Are No Shortcuts* by Rafe Esquith, Pantheon, 2003. 207 pages)

A 'Wife' for all seasons
May 17, 2003

In her robustly satisfying new novel, *The Wife*, Meg Wolitzer throws open the door and invites readers across the threshold smack into the married life of Joe and Joan Castleman.

Even though it is almost impossible to know what goes on inside any marriage, that does not deter one's curiosity. We never stop, figuratively, peering into windows and listening in on conversations, trying to learn through observation. In the case of the Castlemans, Wolitzer makes it easy and delicious to look, listen and, ultimately, to judge.

The vicarious experience is great fun. The Castlemans are like the people one follows in high-toned gossip columns. In fact, this couple seemed so familiar I recently caught myself in mid-sentence, about to ask a friend what Joan Castleman was doing these days. But she is just a fictional character – or is she?

Joe is a renowned novelist, you see, of the post-World War II generation, a large character, famous, conflicted, admired, showered with awards. He is both a literary and commercial success. Think of Norman Mailer, James Jones, Joseph Heller – you get the idea.

"Joan is extremely busy baby-sitting for my ego," Joe jokes to his adoring sycophants. Joanie is his little woman, smiling behind the ficus branches at cocktail parties and soirees, holding the fort at home and trying not to notice the constant trails of sweet, gushing, aspiring female writers who circle her husband.

We are introduced to the Castlemans on their way to Helsinki, Finland, where Joe is to receive a grand literary prize worth about half-a-million dollars, representing the culmination of his eminent career. It seems odd at first that Joan, in this exact moment of triumph, decides to leave Joe. She's had enough.

That Joan is angry and has a right to be is evident. That she also possesses a killer wit and wry sense of humor drives this story into lift-off.

"Every marriage is just two people striking a bargain," Joe tells Joan, in a wheedling attempt to win her back. It turns out a bargain was indeed struck between these two, beginning in a classroom at Smith College in the '50s, which incubated a romantic fantasy between a professor and his flushed and fresh young student. Joan leaves school to follow Joe to New York and a life of helping him realize his potential, a goal for which she is uniquely qualified. Boy, does she help him!

A mystery insinuates itself onto the page, little questions concerning Joe's fabulous talent. One keeps reading, wanting to know more.

Wolitzer is a fine writer who just keeps getting better. She takes her time, allowing her characters to develop real heft as she guides us through the world of New York literary life, territory she knows well. A second-generation writer, daughter of novelist Hilma Wolitzer, she delivers dead-on riffs one does not have to be an insider to appreciate. The lofty readings in academic settings. The testosterone- and ego-driven parties where burly authors spar like mastodons.

I liked particularly a set piece at a fictitious summer writing conference called Butternut Peak but sounding a lot like the famous Bread Loaf. Wolitzer plays wickedly with the idea of pretty but pathetic women who sleep with writers as a path to fame.

Though much of *The Wife* is playful in tone, the author does not ignore the dark corners of the marriage. She renders the effect this bad bargain has on the offspring of the Castleman union with poignant truth. Especially moving is a passage in which Joan imagines telling her daughter why she does not leave her husband, something she cannot "logically explain."

"The husband," Joan thinks. "A figure you never strove toward, never worked yourself up over, but simply lived beside season upon season, which started piling up like bricks spread thick with sloppy mortar."

If there is a dated sound to this, it is because of the specific period Wolitzer chose for her story, a decision absolutely necessary for its success. Joan's choices fit like a glove into this '50s time frame, before women's liberation and equal opportunity and universal frowning on sexual harassment.

Wolitzer manages to modernize her novel in the timeless way she presents marriage itself: how husbands and wives fight, how they deceive themselves in order to endure marriage, how they physically age into what Joan calls "the luxury of the familiar." I loved Joan, even though I wanted to shake some sense into her wise and cute head, asking: Why? Why did you do it? Was it worth all the agony?

Eventually, all the important mysteries are solved except, perhaps, the mystery of why women put up with men at all. I suspect many women will want to plant wet kisses on the page where Joe is pleading for understanding and forgiveness, sort of, and Joan responds with, "You're an enormous baby, that's all you are."

Wolitzer leaves the reader with hope that Joan will receive more than her just reward and a bundle of prize money to boot. This book is definitely on the side of women, if we can still say such a thing in the age of political correctness. I can think of dozens of friends who would love this novel. Alas, none of them are men.

(*The Wife* by Meg Wolitzer. Scribner, 2003. 219 pages)

A 'Walk' worth taking
May 30, 2003

"He just got more and more into his own little world."

Thus Cathryn E. Smith describes her father's slow descent into the cluttered and perilous landscape of Alzheimer's disease. In *The Glory Walk*, she collects conversations, poetry, letters and even dreams to shape an uncommonly appealing memoir of this man's life. A poet herself, Smith infuses what might be an unrelenting dark "walk" with a kind of joyful music and light.

Bob Smith was an ordinary man with a loving wife and three daughters, one of whom "turned out really fine," he would joke. He was a tall man, his daughter writes, "like growing up with the Empire State building, except no elevator or gift shop." He loved to sail boats, taking the whole family along, and grow gorgeous flowers from seed then sit right down on the earth among them.

The courtship of Bob and Judy Smith evokes a period of glamour, of breezing around New York drinking martinis and rum punches. Marriage means the suburbs and children but somehow never settling down to dullness and predictable routine.

Bob Smith is the opposite of drab – a father who wears Mickey Mouse ties and cooks runny poached eggs for his girls when mother is away, who tells amazing stories and trims the Christmas tree without a ladder, who loves to talk and dance and play the piano and manages to get his children to church on time, even when he is painting a room.

How unbelievable when he begins to forget, not just names or dates but how to bend his body to fit into a car. He becomes deaf and quiet or angry and stubborn. With his great strength, he breaks a fellow patient's arm in a care facility.

Smith does not organize her memoir chronologically. In highly successful sections titled Disease-Man, she gets into his increasingly inaccessible head, repeating phrases as he does, re-creating those non-sequiturs and random speech patterns of his illness. We do not learn the dates of her father's birth or exact details of his youth and career. That is all unimportant, as her purpose is not biography. She gets every necessary thing exactly right, such as the "litter-boxy" smell of his room or the way he became a "man-child in a room full of adults."

Almost too poignant to bear is the author's brief description of the last image of her dad. Needing professional care but always wanting to go home, he had to be restrained at leave-takings, strapped into a blue plastic chair. With both tough and tender courage, Cathryn Smith tilts her vision slightly in order to see "a little boy playing spaceman ... waving to the cheering crowd as he prepares to blast off."

Writing about one's father has become a tiny subset of literary genre. Phillip Roth several years ago and Sherwin Nuland and Sue Miller more recently have produced touching books. I would place *The Glory Walk* in their company, even at the head of the line. Smith's poetic precision and creative use of language work to present a small miracle: her father comes alive and is made known to strangers. I grieved honestly for this family's loss, even though there is not a whiff of asking for condolence.

Bob Smith died on March 20, 1991, at 8:10 a.m. with a kind nurse holding his hand, telling him to hold on; his wife was coming.

It happened that I read this work in a sunny garden, sitting about 20 feet from the room where my own father died. I stayed there a long time, feeling grateful for ways to re-connect.

Alfred, Lord Tennyson, wrote "Old men must die; or the world would grow moldy, would only breed the past again." I guess that is so, and he is no doubt wiser than I.

It is certain that through our youth the world stays green and lush. Yet giving up the old often brings up an ache similar to seeing a fine, ancient tree cut down. The life of a vibrant man, even aged, even diseased, is a great force and presence and cannot easily be replaced with something tenuous and unformed. Once gone, he can only be held in memory and shared in words.

The Glory Walk is a gift that must be shared.

(*The Glory Walk: A Memoir* by Cathryn E. Smith. VanderWyk & Burnham, 2003. 208 pages)

The shocking secrets of 'Gender Talk'
June 5, 2003

It is difficult to imagine a more startling thesis in a book about black America than the one stated in *Gender Talk*. Co-authors Johnnetta Betsch Cole and Beverly Guy-Sheftall assert the antagonisms and communication problems between men and women are more damaging to the black community than issues of race alone.

These two women – friends and serious scholars – have produced a book both courageous and informative. They open windows and boldly air their "race's dirty linen" in this meticulously researched and documented work.

When Anita Hill accused Supreme Court nominee Clarence Thomas of sexual harassment in the fall of 1991, the complexities of black gender drew the attention of the whole nation, causing widespread public fascination and confusion. This was something new. It seemed the white community long had assumed a sort of collegiality among blacks.

My personal awakening to the perplexing and complicated nature of black male-female relations came from reading Alice Walker's *The Color Purple*. I never could quite understand the passage where Celie, having suffered continual abuse from both her stepfather and husband, offers such seemingly illogical advice to her stepbrother, Harpo, on how to handle his strongly independent wife, Sofia. Although Celie and Sofia are friends and Harpo possesses a confused sense of his masculinity, she tells him, "Beat her."

In truth, as Cole and Guy-Sheftall reveal, that culture retains a long-held value to close ranks and protect men at all costs. Any black woman who goes against a brother is vilified and scorned. "Thomas's support in the black community actually increased after Hill's charges of sexual misconduct," they write. "He became yet another example of a Black man targeted by the system presumably for sexual crimes he did not commit."

The authors present a credible rationale for the tangled web of black gender issues, going back to the institution of slavery. Enslaved men were so emasculated by white owners and so unable to protect their women that, even in freedom, black women worked overtime to build up, support and defend their men. This attitude has resulted in a patriarchal society, one in which some black men have abused their women and children from a latent need to exert their authority, expressed in bruising hyper-masculinity.

I must say, Cole and Guy-Sheftall tackle some weighty subjects. They examine the black church and its dominance over women, the homophobia rampant among blacks, and the growing problem of HIV/AIDS – now the leading cause of death for black women ages 25 to 44 in the United States. That fact alone shocked me; I wonder if it likewise shocks the women of the black community.

The authors also focus on little-known bits of black cultural history, such as the female lynchings that took place after the Civil War and lasted until the Depression. Nothing they write is meant to be sensational, yet I constantly was jolted into fresh awareness of what they refer to as "intraracial gender matters." They bravely step into the world of hip-hop music and its generally vulgar lyrics, which celebrate men's dominance over and denigration of women. Cole and Guy-Sheftall are genteel, educated women – one a college president, the other a professor and editor – yet they choose to delve into dark spaces in order to expose and possibly correct areas of their culture badly in need of change.

Statistics indicate black women are graduating from college in record numbers and moving into highly paid professional careers. Hollywood presents images of Angela Bassett and Whoopi Goldberg living it up in Jamaica, having it all. Despite these hard-fought gains, the authors detail how black women are losing respect in their own community, are remaining partner-less and suffering from rape and incest in order to prop up black men – and no one wants to talk about it. Silence reigns.

Gender Talk presents many voices along with those of the authors, and the quotations compare with cut crystal, they are so clear. Consider this comment of Byllye Avery: "The number one issue for most of our sisters is violence – battering, sexual abuse."

How pathetic to note the only gender issue discussed ad nauseam in the media today concerns the trivial question of whether a woman golfer should be allowed to compete equally with men. Thank goodness for a strong and growing black intelligentsia in America and for the forum provided by this book to raise difficult but substantive matters. The voices speaking here deserve an audience.

As mentioned, this is a work of impressive scholarship, broadly researched and carefully footnoted. Yet it reads easily and the subject is truly fascinating. The authors weave their arguments from painful human histories. Considering the ongoing disrespect and actual brutality toward black women, I detected no off-putting anger and blame, just refreshing consistency and a clean, proud tone.

Although Cole and Guy-Sheftall offer no easy answers, they do end with humor and hope, recounting advice from an African American brother encouraging them to practice the Noah Principle. "There will be no more credit for predicting the rain," he tells them. "It's time to build the ark."

(*Gender Talk: The Struggle for Women's Equality in African American Communities* by Johnetta Betsch Cole and Beverly Guy-Sheftall. Ballantine Books, 2003. 336 pages)

A dazzling 'Funeral'
June 16, 2003

Not surprising, Benita Eisler begins *Chopin's Funeral*, her melodious narrative of the life of Frederic Chopin, with his death. On a bright October day in 1849, more than 4,000 mourners crammed into the temple-like Church of the Madeleine in Paris to say farewell to the musical genius. The service could not have been more lavish or costly. How ironic for a man who spent his final years in near-isolation from friends and family, scraping out an existence, desperately ill and terrified of becoming destitute.

Although the arc of Chopin's brief but productive life (he died at 39) is well known, Eisler's ability to penetrate the psyches and inner lives of her cast of characters makes this story seem newly gripping and freshly told.

Everything about Chopin's career appears improbable. A small, sickly but talented son of simple Polish parents, he flees his native country as a young man, driven away by his loyalty to the crumbling monarchy. Exiled to Paris, he becomes the darling of the aristocratic classes, depending on their patronage to make his way. Conservative, elegant, diminutive, he ends up in the arms of the most notorious woman of almost any age, six years his senior.

The story of Chopin cannot be disentangled from the life of George Sand, the pants-wearing, cigar-smoking libertine female who shocked even Paris with her multiple love affairs and independent life. The opposite of Chopin politically, she kept company with "sweaty, loud, ill-mannered journalists, organizers, and worker-poets." He craved the concerts, balls and glittering salons of the city. A stylish dandy, barely 5 feet tall, he began a fad for lavender gloves, certain scented soaps and shades of wallpaper. Sand presided over her country house, Nohant, managed her large extended family, sat up all night writing novels and journalistic pieces and still possessed energy to put up 40 pounds of plum jam single-handedly.

Any telling of the romance of these two always centers on the famous Majorcan winter, where they escaped for sunshine and a restoration of Chopin's always-fragile health. They found isolation, constant dreary rain and no servants. Sand, ever rising to the occasion, did the cooking, kept her boy-genius dry and even managed to have a full-sized piano delivered over rocks to their remote location – in tune, yet!

Thus began a period of mutual admiration and care, of ecstatic and tender nurturing of Chopin's art by Sand. "I feel as peaceful as a baby in its cradle," he wrote to a friend.

The problem with any biography of Chopin is the dominance of Sand's character. Yet Eisler admirably manages to keep the focus on Chopin's struggles to teach, compose and perform. He preferred the private concert, subscribed to by friends and devotees. "I am not fit to give concerts," he said. "The crowd intimidates me, and I feel suffocated by its eager breath, paralyzed by its inquisitive stare, silenced by its alien faces."

He seldom could bring himself to play in public. How fortunate were the relatively few people who ever heard him perform his music. All accounts by those who were so blessed rave about his delicate touch, intricate fingering and coaxing of beautiful tone from his large pianoforte. He had a unique way of stroking the keys, causing a note to linger and shimmer a little while before fading away. I kept thinking of Olympic diver Greg Louganis, who would lift off the platform and seem to hang there a moment in perfect form before plunging into the water.

Inevitably, the complex personalities of Sand and Chopin clashed. Each was demanding in different ways. She described it in a thinly disguised *roman à clef* as a "desperate struggle as to which would consume the other." She began to ease her "angel" from her inner circle, banishing him first from Nohant and then breaking finally from their shared quarters in Paris.

The manner in which Sand distanced herself from her formally adored lover can only be described as cruel and insensitive. She showed similar disdain for her daughter, Solange, whose own story, a tragic subplot in this tale, has all the characteristics of Eisler's definition of the "ultimate romantic requirement: beauty touched with strangeness."

The author has a charming way of imagining how music sounds. Writing about the "Third Scherzo in C-sharp minor," for instance, she describes the uncertain rhythms and key as though the composer has opened a lion's cage and is facing down the beast. "Violence is courted," she purrs, "only to be elegantly controlled."

Chopin's loneliness and despair after the brutal separation from Sand, along with a dangerous insurrection in Paris, sent him to England and Scotland in his final year, seeking stipends and pupils, unappreciated and ignored.

An interesting irony is that, 150 years after his death, Chopin's music grows in reputation. He is known and loved and performed and, yes, still mourned. Sand, who outlived him by 26 years, is known mainly for her affair with him. Few of her written works remain in print, and she is largely unread.

I wish so many biographies did not end in sorrow.

Nevertheless, I found this an uplifting book. It might be sacrilegious to say, but a swift portrait of a life, packed with interesting insights and carefully selected details, can be as satisfying as an all-inclusive tome full of documentation and dating every grocer's bill, every appointment and litany of the subject's antecedents. I mean no disrespect to David McCullough, Robert A. Caro and other giant Sequoia biographers, but Benita Eisler's more compact style is dazzling. I will eagerly read anything she writes.

(*Chopin's Funeral* by Benita Eisler. Knopf, 2003. 240 pages)

Falling from the 'Heights'
June 20, 2003

I expected to love Cheryl Mendelson's novel, *Morningside Heights*. Her first book, the surprise best-seller *Home Comforts*, is a guilty pleasure I keep at hand as a guide for restoring order when my household gets a bit out of control. A volume of encyclopedic magnitude, *Home Comforts* details everything one needs to know about making a home. Believe me, it is a gem.

So I curled up with *Morningside Heights* and a cup of herbal tea, longing to sink into that dreamy world of imagination we all need at times – and the best fiction provides. Yet, after what seemed to be hours of giving it a go, I was only on page 31.

Alas, the book is an interminable read.

It should be fun. After all, the setting is a hip and happening neighborhood in New York City that will be familiar to any fan of Jerry Seinfeld. But the author goes overboard, spending pages and more pages in the first chapter hammering home to readers just how interesting and appealing this evolving and gentrified area is. I began to wonder if anyone not actually living there could find it all that fascinating.

The characters are smart, talented and earnest – but, again, so many of them are crammed between these covers it begins to seem like overkill. After a while, I couldn't bear to meet anyone else and hear yet another personal history of someone who, it turns out, did not matter at all in the narrative.

The main plot revolves around Charles and Anne Braithewaite and their complicated family finances. Charles is a singer who, although successful, has never quite reached his full potential. Anne is a fine pianist who gives lessons, accompanies occasionally and dotes on her four children. I know I was supposed to admire Anne as much as the author obviously does, but I found her insufferable.

Anne is the ultimate Earth mother – warm, caring and so politically correct she is "even for free speech for pornographers." She wants only the best for her babies, sending them to expensive private schools and supplying them with fine and costly instruments in order to nurture their musical genius. The Braithwaite household is one of hospitality and largesse, where guests are welcomed to a table set with the finest foods.

Eventually, their profligate spending habits force the Braithwaites to sell their beloved co-op apartment in Morningside Heights and move to the suburbs. Each blames the other and treats this fate as worse than death. Charles even feels like crying at the thought of Westchester or New Jersey. The author extols the glories of the parks, museums, concerts and eclectic mix of people in the city, but the suburbs and small towns upstate are depicted as mediocre and inferior places, graveyards of culture.

When Anne and Charles ultimately escape their destiny of ruin, I did not sigh with relief, because their rescue through sudden wealth seems contrived and undeserved.

During the time of this impending move, the couple is trying to sort out a messy love triangle among their friends Merrit, Morris and Lily. This part is pretty amusing, but in a grim way. I was disappointed to discover that Mendelson, who described her bedroom in *Home Comforts* as "the cave of nakedness," cannot write a decent love scene.

When these characters get together, they do not neck and nuzzle and mutter delicious nothings. Rather, they speak as though they are pulling thick textbooks from the shelves and reading lengthy passages of boring and tedious psychology and philosophy to each other. All of these folks would much prefer debating to kissing and lab work to honest petting. Good heavens! One character is so out of touch with herself that she is five months pregnant before it occurs to her that might be the reason she is gaining weight and feeling ill.

Come to think of it, all the people in this book speak an oddly stilted dialogue – even the children. When was the last time you saw a "besuited businessman" or heard someone "snicker" or "snigger" when talking about love? And do we still refer to someone as "a good egg," let alone "a real sobersides?" Even characters from Edith Wharton's or Henry James's New York sound more up-to-date.

Another whole story line involves Elizabeth Miller, an elderly spinster who lives across the hall from Charles and Anne. Her mysterious death brings a sympathetic priest and a shady lawyer to the scene, along with caregivers, building maintenance staff and half the residents of 635 West 117th Street. Oh, yes, that's another thing. Descriptions are ultra-precise in *Morningside Heights*. About 40 times, someone boards the M4 bus and proceeds cross-town, naming just about every stop. We always learn which subway station or restaurant a character enters. Instead of producing a cheerful intimacy with the neighborhood, this technique is somehow off-putting and repetitious, like reading lists in a catalogue. I've never felt less like exploring a literary landscape.

I still admire Mendelson's previous writing, but it takes more than a contract to turn a successful non-fiction writer into a novelist. With some dismay, I read on the book jacket that this is to be the first volume in a trilogy. Do we really need more about characters whose success lies in "transforming their neurotic misery into ordinary unhappiness?"

Reading *Morningside Heights* is like sitting through six hours of listening to characters moaning, agonizing about their psyches, dissecting each other's thoughts and nervous disorders. In other words, a very long Woody Allen movie without the jokes.

(*Morningside Heights: A Novel* by Cheryl Mendelson. Random House, 2003. 336 pages)

Walking 'Hallowed Ground'
June 26, 2003

If James McPherson were a Civil War tour guide, he would rank as a general. After reading his enthralling *Hallowed Ground*, in which he leads his readers through the three-day battle of Gettysburg, it is almost a demotion to say he is a professor at

Princeton and one of our greatest living historians. So comfortable, confident and alive is his circuit of the famous battlefield that even though I have visited there many times, I wanted to jump in my car and head immediately for Pennsylvania.

It is the gift of a true historian to make old, familiar events and places spring fresh into one's mind. Although this clash of Union and Confederacy remains, as the author states, the "largest battle ever fought in the Western Hemisphere," and though books on this subject could fill whole libraries – let alone its many depictions in film – McPherson's skilled retelling sets a new standard for compactness and clarity.

Hallowed Ground is the latest offering from Crown Publishing in its series called Crown Journeys. I have grown fond of these succinct volumes and their elegant format. Similar to the lively biographies published by Penguin, these volumes are likewise written by famous authors who possess an affinity for or association with their subjects.

Depending on the artistry of the individual author, each book can seem like a worthy but mere introduction to the topic or a complete and satisfying rendering. McPherson is the latter type.

His tone is unaffected and his method is simple. He begins by placing the reader "three miles northwest of the Gettysburg town square" and then proceeds to walk one, literally, over the course of troop movements, where the generals placed their headquarters, the scenes of major skirmishes and conflicts and where horses and men fell in "concentrated carnage." Along the way, he points out monuments, observation towers and landmarks existing today but not on July 1, 1863. He speaks of orchards and farmhouses since lost. His remarkable ability to skim deftly along present surfaces as he recreates those agonizing days is a joy, if I may say such a thing about so tragic an event.

McPherson knows this terrain well, having led countless groups of students and scholars over its contours. His familiarity with the ground is matched by his ease with all the players – the officers and soldiers who believed in separate "causes," enough to fight and die for. His recounting of Pickett's famous charge – the "high-water mark of the Confederacy" – and the way he tries to grasp why men will walk into an artillery barrage across open land, is especially wonderful.

It is always difficult to understand why wars begin. McPherson does not tackle that greater subject in this book, as he has in many others. He focuses on this one battle, one he calls a "meeting engagement." It was not necessarily supposed to happen in Gettysburg. No strategic advantage would go to either army in victory – no river or city or store of munitions.

McPherson sums up the reason for the battle taking place in rural Pennsylvania this way: "Lee decided to carry the war into Pennsylvania in a bid to conquer a peace on northern soil." Coming off a big Confederate victory at Chancellorsville two months previously, Lee saw no reason the pattern could not repeat in Yankee territory. So the armies met where roads conveniently led – roads, it turns out, that were crucial. Helpful maps, printed on the book's end papers, show just where tiny Gettysburg sits – as the center of a spoke of roads and pikes, facilitating easy movement of men and heavy equipment.

I marveled at all the individual stories and fascinating details McPherson manages to include in this pithy volume. He explains why one hoof or two is lifted on equestrian statues, how General Custer led a charge of Michigan Wolverines, what was going on with Lee's digestive tract and why President Lincoln did not send his letter of congratulation to General Meade. He debunks several famous myths about the fight, such as the one about the Blues and Grays drinking from the same stream.

McPherson also puts to rest the persistent rumor that he is descended from the respected young general James Birdseye McPherson, a good friend of U. S. Grant. How unfortunate – I always liked that one.

For many years, McPherson has been active in efforts to preserve the battlefields of the Civil War. He writes of the aftermath, when various regiments and groups sought to erect monuments glorifying their valiant acts and how sometimes further battles ensued over these issues. As he guides us over the arena of combat, he comments on how this scene was played in such-and-such movie or in so-and-so's novel. He nudges us to climb the towers, gaze out to the ridges and swells of land, to picture a line of soldiers a mile long emerging from a wood. As he is doing all this, he makes perfect sense of a complex and messy process, both presenting it raw and serving it up neat.

There is a sweep and density to this work that belies its brevity. The heat and humidity outside my window on this late June day call to mind the atmosphere of those dreadful mornings and afternoons, three wretched days that changed the course of a war and of this nation. It is important to remember what happened there, as Lincoln eloquently prompted us to do.

As long as James McPherson can hold a pen, memory will live.

(*Hallowed Ground: A Walk at Gettysburg* by James M. McPherson. Crown Journeys, 2003. 144 pages)

Happily recalling 'All That'
July 8, 2003

As they say in the movies, the couple met "cute."

She was a barely-16-year-old schoolgirl dancing in a chorus on Broadway as a summer job before college. She mistook him for a busboy, not realizing he was the show's choreographer, dashing, handsome and 12 years her senior.

In a little over a year, Betsy Blair became Mrs. Gene Kelly. If this story had a typical Hollywood ending, they would have danced their way to fame and fortune and a happily-ever-aftering life. But as Blair tells us in *The Memory of All That*, a more bittersweet fate awaited her.

The early romance between Blair and one of America's most famous song-and-dance men cries out to be acted on the silver screen. To be young and beautiful and in love in New York, dancing up a storm and staying up to all hours – who could ask for anything more? Somehow, reading Blair's story, lyrics from all the old love songs come to mind. Yet her writing is anything but cliched or rehashed.

One of the true pleasures of reading this book is listening to Blair's voice, absorbing her intelligence, originality and natural honesty. Her work does not sound ghost-written, nor does it possess that "as-told-to" tedium. Her prose spills onto the page with a kind of bounce, as though she is living her experience again as she writes and seeing her life with fresh vision.

And what a life! She married Kelly on the eve of World War II, but that did not mar their happiness. Happiness is expressed throughout the book, recounting her childhood and marriage and afterward. "We ate when we were hungry," she writes, as they started out on their honeymoon. "We made love wherever we were, we drove through the night if we felt like it ... I wasn't surprised by all this freedom and joy."

They drove to Hollywood and set up housekeeping in a charming farmhouse on Rodeo Drive. At that time, a bridle trail ran down the middle of the road, but no one was ever seen on horseback. Kelly was just getting started at MGM, creating the great musicals of his brilliant career. In fact, their life there sounds like a musical. Blair remembers "California sunshine and flowers, a great daughter, a happy house overflowing with love and fun and friends, and no worry about money – all this stemmed from Gene's work."

She would take her daughter, Kerry, to school in the morning as Adolph Green and Betty Comden were arriving at the house to work on some great show such as "Singin' in the Rain." Leonard Bernstein insisted they buy a new piano for their constant parties, and he spent an entire day choosing the perfect one for them. She had a gardener, a cook and a housekeeper. She could buy anything she wanted or do whatever she wished.

One thing she did was act occasionally. She had an unusual quality on the screen – not quite the young ingenue but something edgier. She looked sweet with her creamy skin and voluminous red hair, yet she chose parts with depth and complexity. Her greatest performance came when she won the role of Clara in the film "Marty" with Ernest Borgnine. A beautiful young woman in reality, for the character she became a shy, repressed teacher who falls in love with an overweight butcher. The movie, of course, won the Academy Award for Best Picture in 1955.

It was a perfect life with nothing exactly wrong or bad. Yet Blair was experiencing what uber-feminist Betty Friedan would later call "the problem that has no name." It is the problem that exists for women whose identity somehow gets lost in marriage.

Betsy still loved Gene, but "it was his life that I was becoming part of, not my life nor even our life, but his." Something had to happen. She began having small affairs. "I spent my whole adolescence as a married woman and was completely happy," she writes. "The inevitable forces of nature, growth and rebellion were postponed. But they came later."

When those forces arrived, she found herself in love with another man. She left her marriage and Hollywood and took her daughter to live in Paris. She experienced a "mysterious feeling of relief, of serenity, even," she says.

Surprising, but at this point, her story becomes even more fascinating. As she faded away from the movie and celebrity scene, she came alive in Europe, acting with famous and difficult directors, becoming more active in leftist politics and allowing herself fulfillment as a woman. She speaks with candor and with complete kindness toward her lovers and family. This lady became a real grownup.

Blair eventually married again, not to the runaway Paris lover, but to director Karel Reisz. She has known many fascinating and famous people whom she describes in illustrative vignettes. She takes full responsibility for her choices, saying, "I paid a price for my good life." By the end, my imaginary background music had shifted from "Me and My Gal" to Edith Piaf's "*Je ne regret rien.*"

Blair has written a terrific book. She captures an era along with her own life. I've added her to my ever-growing list of people with whom I'd love to have dinner. She manages to put an honest face on a fairy tale marriage without spoiling it. There is one fabulous scene in which she, Kelly and their daughter dance across a street in London while a crowd serenades them with "Singin' in the Rain." If life could always be like that!

Several weeks before I read this book, I happened to catch "Marty" on the Turner Classic Movies channel. I was struck by Blair's strong performance, by what a nuanced, fine actress she is. It's ironic that such a beautiful, sexy, interesting woman is best known for playing the consummate, homely wallflower.

I also thought: "Marty" is a perfect movie. I hope no one ever gets the dumb idea to remake it.

(*The Memory of All That: Love and Politics in New York, Hollywood and Paris* by Betsy Blair. Knopf, 2003. 352 pages)

Heroic and human 'John Paul Jones'
July 15, 2003

It is three o'clock in the afternoon of September 23, 1779. Captain of the Continental Navy John Paul Jones sights *HMS Serapis*, a British man-of-war, about 10 miles away, off the east coast of England. Jones's ship, the clumsy and slow *Bonhomme Richard*, prepares for battle. Sailors scatter sand on the deck to prevent slipping in blood. Surgeons belowdecks set out tubs to receive amputated limbs.

No American ship had ever defeated a British ship of any size. Yet Jones makes ready and steers right for the enemy, drawing within "a pistol shot." Thus begins Evan Thomas's exhaustive but thrilling biography, *John Paul Jones: Sailor, Hero, Father of the American Navy*." Evans sets the scene with maximum suspense but then makes a reader wait for nearly 200 pages to discover the outcome of that great engagement at sea.

In the meantime, we learn about this prickly, ambitious man and his struggle to earn command of a worthy battleship, a man whose vision and long-range strategizing ultimately shaped our modern navy. Born in Scotland, perhaps the illegitimate son of the estate where his father was employed as chief gardener, Jones pulled himself up by sheer determination, making himself literate and studying the ways of gentlemen.

Leaving his native country under a cloud and gaining sea experience any way he could – even by commanding a slave ship – Jones worked his way to America just at the moment of its Revolution. With Britain utterly owning the seas and the Continental Congress at odds over the "madness" of even attempting to float a Navy, there was great leeway for advancement in a practically nonexistent fleet.

After turning an old merchant ship, the *Alfred*, into a clumsy man-of-war, Jones was present at the very first landing of the Continental Marines in Nassau in 1776 and, later that same year, engaged in the first real naval battle of the new nation off Block Island, south of Rhode Island. Although this was reported to be a victory for the Americans, circumstances were such that Congress immediately ordered an investigation – another first for the fledgling nation.

But Jones had found a place to excel. He possessed good instincts and a fearless impatience for battle. Longing for a fast ship, he wrote for posterity: "I intend to go in harm's way." It was to be the bane of his career that he never did achieve command of a swift, maneuverable vessel, yet he did go in harm's way – again and again. During his next command in the Providence, he developed his "saucy" style of taunting enemy ships and tricking them with unexpected moves and ploys, much the way other American revolutionaries were fighting on land.

Leading up to his great battle with the *Serapis*, Jones built a reputation for going into the face of the enemy, scuttling into British territory and terrorizing the civilian population as well as combatants. Even in these early stages of modern combat, Jones understood the "power of psychological warfare," of threatening the complacency of the English and their formerly impregnable coastlines. In this, he was a noble antecedent to General U.S. Grant in the Civil War. Grant, too, was a fighter who dove behind hostile lines to bring the war home to the South.

I found significant pleasure in reading this book from Thomas's own comfort with the sensations of being on the water and his ease with marine vocabulary. I was reminded frequently of the giddy happiness expressed by the good-natured Water Rat in Kenneth Graeme's *The Wind in the Willows* and his love of "messing around in boats." Thomas includes a helpful glossary, but it is seldom necessary to use this reference, as his descriptions flow in such a way that one stays in the grip of the action.

And what action he gives us! The finest passages are those of battle and Jones' incredible mind and physical stamina under pressure. Plagued with mutinous and inexperienced crews, with sullen and inferior officers and with his own limitations as a leader of men, nevertheless Jones excelled in battle. In fact, Thomas tells us, "Mortal peril seems to have lightened Jones' step, made him more clever and nimble." He writes of the "savage joy that seized him at moments of maximum peril." Jones simply never gave up. In the throes of his most famous clash with the *Serapis*, he managed to bind the two ships together in a "desperate clinch" and fire away until they were both burning. Jones probably never did utter the phrase: "I have not yet begun to fight." Still, it was Captain Pearson who struck his colors at last and called surrender.

The accounts of Jones's stunning victory over the *Serapis*, an earlier engagement between his ship *Ranger* and the British *HMS Drake*, and a later frightening voyage in the ship *Ariel* off the Brittany coast – a cruise that reads like *The Perfect Storm* – are worth any amount of plodding through Jones's messy and, at times, pathetic personal life. He seems never to have made one close friend or enjoyed a lasting, loving relationship. Thomas calls him a self-made man, a label that would become closely identified with the new America.

The Founders did not quite know what to do with Jones or how to employ him as a naval officer, a great loss to the country in many ways. His intrepid character was at odds with his personality. He was, truly, a loner whose life was at sea. Like many actors, he did not know how to behave when he was offstage, how to fit in with regular life. He spent his final years commanding a ship for Empress Catherine the Great of Russia and falling foolish victim to the unsavory wiles of Prince Potemkin. Thomas does not labor over Jones's final years but moves prudently to his rather ignominious end in a room in Paris in 1792 at age 45.

It took many years, until July 1905, for Jones to be properly entombed beneath the chapel at the Naval Academy in Annapolis. His reputation is secure, and his exploits and his strategic plans for America to become a maritime power are respected. Thomas steers the story of this complex individual and his interesting era into a safe harbor.

(*John Paul Jones: Sailor, Hero, Father of the American Navy* by Evan Thomas. Simon & Schuster, 2003. 400 pages)

James Wood, critic, tries a novel. Pity.
July 20, 2003

James Wood is a brilliant literary critic. He reads closely and with such dedication and love that his commentary has become a necessity for truly understanding rich literary work. He has the ability to open a reader's mind to new interpretations and possibilities in books familiar or whip up desire to tackle something just published.

Whenever I read a James Wood essay, I immediately want to dip into the book under discussion – even if I have already and recently finished it. That happened last year after I read his superlative review of *Atonement* by Ian McEwan. So penetrating was Wood's analysis, I believed I had not really appreciated the work properly the first time.

When I found his passage on *Moby Dick*, saying Melville wrote the novel that is "every writer's dream of freedom, it was as if he painted a patch of sky for the imprisoned," I dove for my tattered copy and began again that bumpy voyage of Ahab's obsession.

So it was exciting to hear Wood had written a novel at last, a work greatly anticipated by his loyal followers, myself among them. Eagerly, I read the first line: "I denied my father three times, twice before he died, once afterwards."

Uh-oh. Then again, what did I expect from a volume titled *The Book Against God*?

This would be a fine first novel – if written by a just-graduated-from-university student. Then I would call it promising and satisfying. But because the author is a mature, luminous writer who has proved his talent repeatedly, I found the effort disappointing.

The novel fairly reeks with cleverness. Wood demonstrates his skill with polished sentences and apt descriptions. One cannot help being in awe of this man's power with language. I do wish, however, he possessed similar power in simply telling a story.

The story in question is of Thomas Bunting, a somewhat aimless young man who likes "beautiful objects, rich foods, rare atmospheres." Thomas does not have much to show for his years in school. In his late 20s, he works sporadically on his Ph.D. dissertation and reads philosophy, filling notebooks with jottings he calls his "bag," or book against God.

Thomas, you see, is the son of Peter Bunting, an Anglican priest, a gem of a father and quite a perfect man, beloved by his parishioners in a small village in northern England. Thomas' parents are a most affectionate and endearing couple. Although Thomas experienced a wonderful and loving childhood and now is married to Jane, a slightly older and beautiful pianist, he is not happy. He agonizes about his faith, about why, if God exists, He allows humankind to suffer. He has not openly told his parents about his lapsed state and has developed a persistent habit of lying as a form of power.

A crisis occurs when Peter collapses with a heart attack, allowing Thomas to return home – back to the womb so to speak – and deal with his conflicted inner self. That he learns some useful things, yet is still unable to resolve the trouble with the unbelievably patient Jane, pretty much sums up the novel's action. The characters, although well-drawn, seem to gather mostly for the purpose of giving long-winded speeches on esoteric topics: music, Biblical passages, theology in general and death, none of which affect their lives or futures.

Not that there's anything wrong with that, as Jerry Seinfeld would say. It's just that we who love good writing and literature also long for something known as a plot, a storyline. Isn't something supposed to be at stake for the characters? Must it be all about inner meanderings of distressed souls and immature emotional crises?

In his only other published long work, *The Broken Estate*, Wood includes, written in his usual stellar fashion, a critique of Jane Austen. Now there is a literary author who knew how to create a real plot, filled with the tension of a good mystery. Using shapely sentences and dialogue sharpened to diamond-hard precision, Austen threw her delicate heroines into breathless and authentic peril. Love and money, she wrote of her novels, on a one-inch strip of ivory. From that narrow subject matter, she created huge consequences of great importance for Elizabeth or Eleanor or Fanny. Only a heartless reader would stop turning pages before her young men and women are delivered to their inevitable fates.

It is difficult to cheer for Wood's hero. He does not bathe often or change his clothes. He allows his wife to support him, and his thesis languishes in a box while he scribbles useless insights. Peter, his father, is indeed a god-figure. I, for one, cannot imagine a better portrait of an omniscient God, a father both stern and loving, intellectual yet in touch with the common man.

Novels, however, are not paintings hanging on a wall. We need to enter them, walk around in them, not just gaze at their imagery. No doubt Wood's fine mind and sensibilities are on display here, his wit and his affection for the written word. Yet something is lacking.

He ends his novel with a soothing passage describing Thomas listening to a recording of a pianist playing Beethoven. On the record, Thomas hears another sound along with the melody. It is the pianist breathing. Wood calls it, this man's ordinary breathing, "our colorless wind of survival, the zephyr of it all." It is the sound of a man grappling with the sweetness of the music, the sound of hard work, "of existence itself."

That is what is missing in *The Book Against God* – that breath of life, of sweetness. One of the great pleasures of reading is to sense a story breathing and – as so often happens when two happy souls sit closely together – begin to breathe with it as one.

(*The Book Against God: A Novel* by James Wood. Farrar, Straus and Giroux, 2003. 257 pages)

Go fly a kite, Mr. Franklin
August 4, 2003

Has there ever been a more famous or vivid image of a scientific experiment than Benjamin Franklin standing in a thunderous storm, conducting electricity through the string of his homemade kite? Franklin wrestles the kite in a blowing wind, a bolt of lightning strikes a spark and a new chapter in the history of science begins.

The ingenuity, cleverness and daring of Franklin's kite is a solid, original ingredient of our American heritage. How many young people have stood in the rain, kites aloft, keys dangling from string, trying to duplicate the thrill of Franklin when he wrote of receiving the "electric fire freely" as it "streamed out plentifully from the key on the approach of your knuckle"?

In his (pardon me) electrifying book, *Bolt of Fate*, Tom Tucker writes convincingly that Franklin never did, in fact, conduct this experiment. He even goes so far as to call Franklin's claim a hoax. What a shock, that this iconic image – the only scientific experiment ever printed on U.S. currency – might be false.

This is not a comprehensive biography of Franklin. For his complete history, it would be better to read Walter Isaacson's current offering, *Benjamin Franklin*. Tucker, a writer concerned with the history of invention, is interested in Franklin as a scientist with a playful streak. After all, he lived during the Age of Reason, when man was struggling to understand natural phenomena through the collection of empirical data. Any individual who could demonstrate mastery over a deadly natural force such as lightning might be considered truly powerful and god-like.

Tucker wonderfully illuminates details of early experiences with electricity. In the mid-18th century, electricity almost replaced dancing as an entertainment at fashionable parties. Suspending young women on silken cords or standing a dozen soldiers in a line and causing them to receive jolts of static electricity was all the rage. Appreciative audiences ranged from royalty to common folk. Electric shows were hawked at carnivals for cheap thrills. In the meantime, real scientists worked to understand the properties of electricity, and whether the static electricity produced by rubbing glass in elegant parlors was the same force as a bolt of lightning.

Sometime in the summer of 1752, Franklin, a prosperous printer from Philadelphia, published a letter describing his experience of crafting a kite from a single silk handkerchief, getting it soaked in a fierce rainstorm and receiving a shock from a house key that hung on the kite string. He assured his readers that "anyone may try it." The simplicity and homely beauty of this act – serious science "carried out with a child's toy" – attracted the attention of even the mighty Royal Society of London, the premier body of eminent scientific thought and erudition. Franklin had long wished to get the attention of these learned gentlemen and win recognition as a man of science.

Yet would he actually perpetrate a fraud in order to gain international renown, this man of great wit who already enjoyed celebrity and a high standing in his community?

Apparently so. If you follow Tucker's reasoning, it's difficult to conclude otherwise. Tucker examines each assertion of Franklin's and posits the probable truth: Franklin was smart enough to figure out it would work, yet the lack of proper documentation alone would lead one to doubt he actually tried it. It seems Franklin was quite a hoaxer, inventing stories for his newspaper and sometimes using his clever deceptions to get back at people in disputes. In the case of the kite, he might have gone beyond a mere good joke.

Tucker writes at length about one man who quite possibly was a tragic victim of Franklin's alleged deceit. One year later, in 1753, Georg Rikhman, a professor in St. Petersburg, Russia, set up a contraption in his study to receive lightning bolts. With great excitement during a particularly raging storm, he crossed the room toward his desk and was killed instantly by a 15-million-volt lightning strike. The horrific death of this good man received worldwide attention.

Franklin stated in print that Rikhman died because he didn't quite know what he was doing. Tucker speculates that Franklin might have felt some private remorse and helped the deceased professor's children with their educations. The point is, fooling around with lightning was not some parlor trick but a dangerous and potentially deadly endeavor.

Tucker makes the case that because of Franklin's fame with his kite, the Continental Congress sent him to France as goodwill ambassador to enlist support for the revolt against England. The scientific-minded French were especially enthralled with the romantic and sensuous qualities of electric thrills. Franklin's success in winning the favor of Louis XVI was so great that Tucker concludes this story of the kite may well have been "the hoax that won the American Revolution."

Although I cannot fully agree with that surmise – winning American independence was a victory of many parts – Tucker has written a provocative bit of history in amiable style. Franklin was a complex human being and lived in interesting times; his character here is a mere sketch. Yet Tucker includes all that is necessary. He writes like a scientist who enjoys both poetry and a good laugh. Come to think of it, he would have been right at home in the 18th century.

One application of Franklin's "experiment" still in use today is the lightning rod. I found myself thinking of how we have "tamed" this phenomenon – the lightning bolt that regularly burned houses and barns and humans. Now, it is more likely that we fear the loss of electricity, of our power grids failing and plunging us into darkness without heat or air conditioning or television. A quaint parlor game has become a necessity of life.

Bolt of Fate ends with the author paying homage to Franklin by visiting his grave in Philadelphia. I paid tribute by making a cup of tea and turning on my computer and appreciating the great minds whose flair and dedication and courage have provided creature comfort and pleasure to succeeding generations.

(*Bolt of Fate: Benjamin Franklin & His Electric Kite* Hoax by Tom Tucker. Public Affairs, 2003. 297 pages)

Food writer becomes 'Ambulance Girl'
September 10, 2003

I became acquainted with Jane Stern's work a couple of decades ago when, while driving cross-country, I happened to pick up a copy of her delightful book *Road Food*, which she co-authored with her husband, Michael. Perhaps it was the loneliness of the particular trail I was traveling, but I bonded with the Sterns, imagined them to be a fascinating couple full of wit and adventure – and great suggestions as to where to find a decent meal in the boondocks.

Over the years, my interest in the Sterns deepened when I chanced upon one of their columns for Gourmet magazine or heard their jolly commentaries on NPR. They appeared to lead charmed and fruitful lives, and I admit to envying what always seemed to be their breezy and effortless success.

After reading Jane's new book, *Ambulance Girl*, a solo endeavor, I shall never think of them in that old way again. For she reveals her struggle with mid-life depression and its corrosive effect on her marriage. Her husband had his own problems with alcoholism yet managed to remain supportive – up to a point.

Jane followed an unusual path to wellness and strength: She became an emergency medical technician, an EMT.

It is difficult to explain just how engrossing this book is, because often it can be so dull to read about the morass and symptoms of depression, of phobias and fears. It is – depressing.

I puzzled at first as to why I was rapidly turning pages, gulping my way through this personal saga. Stern is not a brilliant, lyrical writer, and her story certainly cannot be universally applied to anyone who is middle-aged or mentally ill.

In the simplest terms, Stern tells an honest story. She never flinches, and I found truth on every page. Truth laced with humor, it turns out, is gripping.

Stern enjoyed a comfy and privileged life in a yellow house on a hill in the small town of Georgetown, Connecticut, an hour and a half from New York City. She and her husband owned and rode horses, had beloved large dogs but no children. They traveled, they schmoozed with editors and agents; they ate fabulous food. But something happened to Stern. She became lifeless and inert, stopped fighting off her obsessions and fears and, eventually, they won the battle.

No longer the traveler, she could not tolerate being on an airplane or even a bus. She went nowhere unless absolutely forced. She stopped caring about her appearance and gained weight – standard stuff for the clinically depressed.

This is where her story takes an odd turn. Stern liked helping people. Almost the only thing that animated her days was the call of a needy soul. So despite her advancing age, her fear of getting into ambulances and her tendency to retch at the sight of blood or other unpleasant bodily excretions, she decides to train as an EMT and learn how to perform difficult rescues in real time.

As someone who has had a number of personal experiences with EMTs "on the scene," so to speak, I must say I had no idea of the rigorous training it takes to become certified. I also do not know how Stern achieved her status. She states unequivocally: "I was never a fan of emergencies of any nature. If there was an accident on the highway, I tucked my head in my hands and didn't look. I feared death and disfigurement. I did not want to see pain or blood or broken glass."

Yet Stern does brave the sight of blood and muck and worse. She goes from sleeping 18 hours a day to pulling herself from sleep at 2 a.m. to yank on overalls, slap a blue light on her car and careen down the highway, answering a 911 call to whatever slaughter or mayhem awaits. She eats doughnuts in the early dawn with other first responders and becomes part of an exclusive club, the members of which are mostly buff young men who fight fires.

Stern writes with insight about the people who really make life in her town work. She once lived on a sort of rarefied fringe, drinking expensive coffees and dropping in at the bookstore. Now, she attends the monthly meetings at the firehouse, rolls hoses and cleans trucks. She sees how the guys who own the gas station and the citizens who staff the local hospital – many of them almost invisible to her formerly – take on huge responsibilities to maintain the safety and health of the community. She becomes part of this working body and, in a personal triumph, earns their respect.

I read *Ambulance Girl* between the recent Labor Day celebration and the upcoming commemoration of the second anniversary of September 11, 2001. The book touches on both events. Stern celebrates work. She draws a clear line between her somewhat fussy former existence and the real challenges of swift reaction to disaster. This requires continual training, drill and a cool head. No time off. She describes her own September 11 experience and how the EMTs in her squad were employed during the terrible days.

I think the word that comes closest to defining the importance of this book is relevance. Relevance to the times we live in, to our messed-up-but-eternally-fixable lives and to the folk who do the truly difficult yet essential jobs.

If I have any complaint at all, it is one Stern makes herself. She writes about how EMTs seldom know the outcome, the end of a story. Their duties draw them to an intersection with lives in trauma and tumult. They help their charges to the next stage and then move on. I found myself wanting to hear more about the man whose dog drowned and who was afraid to tell his partner. Or the lady who grew disgusting herbs and dosed herself with blobs of goo. Though I wished for a bit of closure, I understand how providing this would not be true to the nature of Stern's office.

I finished the book feeling humble and grateful. I was also smiling. Jane Stern dishes up an amazing concoction – a story of real people who teach school, put out blazes, change your oil and oh, by the way, scrape more than blown tires off the road in the middle of the night. Be glad they are out there. Be very glad and proud.

(*Ambulance Girl: How I Saved Myself by Becoming an EMT* by Jane Stern. Crown Publishers, 2003. 240 pages)

'Candy' is dandy
September 22, 2003

Sometimes a book drops into your lap the way a friend unexpectedly offers you a bite of Snickers. That's the way it felt when I read the first few chapters of Hilary Liftin's *Candy and Me*. Although no more than a confection, this book is a sweet diversion from all the serious issues of the day, a welcome bon-bon in a sometimes cauliflower world.

Perhaps I'm just tired of hearing about everyone being on a diet. I have been to gatherings where that is practically the only subject of conversation. Atkins or South Beach. Weight Watchers or Jenny Craig. And scary headlines appear almost every day about how our nation is becoming out of shape and overweight. It's kind of nice to read about Circus Peanuts and Skittles and remember how it was to be a kid and not worry about waistlines.

Liftin takes the subject of candy seriously – in an amusing way. "Candy is a food group," she breezily declares. At first, I could not believe anyone would think this obsessively and constantly about various forms of colored sugar. Yet she began to win me over, especially when she describes a new way to enjoy Hershey Kisses, my personal choice for guilty indulgence.

This book is as unaffected and cheerful as a bowl of bright M&Ms. Each chapter is a brief little nibble, easily gobbled and leaving a pleasant aftertaste. Liftin's story is told simply and rather beautifully. She tells her readers about her love of candy, the ways she prefers to eat candy and how she and candy have interacted through romances and life experiences both painful and delicious.

That's about it. Except along the way, I became acquainted with someone I think would be fun to hang out with – especially when she dismisses tooth decay, weight gain, acne and diabetes with, "I don't want to talk about any of those things." That's what I like about Liftin's approach. This is not about universal cravings and the social implications of addictive habits. She writes about the fun of going into a candy store, about the anticipation of picking out all sorts of treats that are not really good for you.

In passages that recall moments of sharing sweets with friends, Liftin can almost sound like a Seinfeld character, so detailed and filled with minutiae are her descriptions. She makes George Costanza, railing about the supposed theft of his Twix bar, seem almost sane by comparison. In fact, after a while, this bonding over candy and basing whole relationships on similar tastes appears completely normal, certainly no stranger than people, like me, who connect over movies or favorite works of literature.

Liftin is especially good at using particular candies as metaphors, such as the Internet relationship that was "simple, elegant," but not destined to last much longer than a single cinnamon-flavored fireball. A relationship that is going in a "brilliant new direction" is helped along by sharing white chocolate peanut butter cups, a candy that likewise moves in an unexpected direction.

Liftin comes by her habit, as she says, honestly. Her mother had a fierce sweet tooth, which she managed to keep fairly hidden from her daughter. Other family members possessed the same "gene." As a young child, Liftin was stealing candy from her brother and figuring out ways to eat ice cream from the carton and not have it show. She really worked at it.

"In my youth and adolescence, candy was an overindulgence – a mild drug with which I experimented and to which I became addicted. At times it was a substitute for the sweetness and contentedness that I found elusive," she writes. It is not unusual for someone to dose a case of loneliness or awkwardness with an easy sugar rush. Yet the quantities of candy that this author confesses to consuming are startling. It almost staggers one's imagination to contemplate her eating entire bags of conversation hearts before lunch or handfuls of powdered cocoa.

One charming aspect of Liftin's love for candy is her loyalty to frosting, fudge and marshmallow eggs. She never refines her palate or graduates to sophisticated Godiva but remains in that never-never land of gooey, sticky, ultra-sugary childhood fantasy: cotton candy, Twizzlers and Necco wafers.

I kept thinking how lucky she was. She admits that, certainly for a long period of time, her metabolism "was still doing me a few favors. My stomach was flat. My clothes fit me. I was neither thrilled with my body nor unhappy enough to sacrifice candy." A fortunate young lady, indeed. Try as they might, her parents never could get her to eat real fruit; yet she ate pounds of Jelly

Belly beans and other fruit-flavored delights and stayed thin. Why should she change?

As adulthood crept up on her, artificial sweets did not quite satisfy all her longings, and Liftin began to think more about her mental and physical health. She altered her eating patterns and made better choices. Just as in the best of fairy tales, she kisses a few frogs before Prince Charming makes an appearance. He is savvy enough to hide an engagement ring in a pack of Bottle Caps. A perfect match!

I liked Liftin's smarts and honesty, and I genuinely cheered her happy ending. There's no real moral to this story or even any compelling reason to read it. Yet, more than most books, I'd like to share this one with friends. It's bliss – like sharing a box of Junior Mints at the movies. Every day is filled with meat and potatoes, with vegetables and wheat germ. What's wrong with a little dessert?

(*Candy and Me: A Love Story* by Hilary Liftin. Free Press, 2003. 224 pages)

What some people do 'in the Name of God'
October 21, 2003

How many times have we been told that the Bible supplies passages in support of whatever point of view or behavior one wishes to follow? This appears to be true of the Quran as well.

Throughout the world, certain individuals – acting alone or as a member of a cult organization – are committing crimes and acts of terror and are convinced they do so with God's approval and blessing.

"Religious terrorism arises from pain and loss and from impatience with a God who is slow to respond to our plight, who doesn't answer."

So begins Jessica Stern's book *Terror in the Name of God*, an attempt to come to grips with people who righteously kill and maim.

This is a scholarly work with a sort of popular overlay consisting of riveting passages detailing Stern's interviews with actual terrorists, at times conducted on their turf. I finished reading the book with two definite impressions of the author: She is exceptionally bright and uncommonly courageous.

Stern's book is the account of her personal journey from merely studying chemical warfare and terrorism to traveling to at least six countries for the purpose of interviewing terrorists – sometimes in dangerous situations. As a result of her efforts, she can offer much to our collective struggle in trying to understand the minds of individuals who, as she states, "profess to have moral values" yet "do evil things."

Understanding and information are what Stern is after. She carefully lays out her motives for becoming involved in risky behaviors. Brought up in a secular Jewish home, she wants to penetrate the mysteries of faith and even professes to envying the strong and certain faith of a violent apocalyptic terrorist, Kerry Noble, "even as I was horrified by his cult's plots and crimes."

This is no light or easy read. Stern's research is comprehensive, and her personal experiences punctuate and illuminate her theses. She begins, interestingly enough, by describing her interviews with American Christian terrorists, members of the cult CSA – the Covenant, the Sword and the Arm of the Lord. The group focused on hastening the return of the Messiah by causing Armageddon on Earth in the form of poisoning or eliminating in other ways Jews, blacks, homosexuals and socialists. They also amassed huge stocks of weapons with which to "carry out God's judgments."

CSA remains an active conspiracy group. Kerry Noble, a reformed CSA member who has served time in prison, says of another, still-active member, that he becomes agitated at signs of the coming Apocalypse and "Any sign that he sees could make him turn violent."

Stern has organized her work into two parts. The first discusses root causes for terrorism, such as alienation, humiliation or territory. The second describes how terrorist groups are formed and operate. In this section, I found her experience with the recently executed Presbyterian minister Paul Hill of particular interest.

Hill is what Stern calls "an inspirational leader." He led an effort to stop abortion, what he calls "the innocent unborn," by encouraging his followers to fight this scourge as people fought Hitler's killing of Jews. He sees this as a moral equivalent and died by lethal injection for his murder of an abortion doctor and a security guard.

Stern is excellent at explaining how men like Hill inspire a "congregation," as in a "normal" religion. But unlike most religions, she states, the aim of these leaders is to "inspire followers to take violent action on behalf of the in-group in opposition to an out-group."

That sums up what happens worldwide with these organizations. Wherever Stern travels, she finds the terrorists' emphasis to be on taking violent action. From Arkansas and Florida to Pakistan and Kashmir, she talks to individuals waging their jihads or crusades and discovers similarities of intent, methods of operation and fundraising.

Basically, the groups are funded through a network of "charities." The people at the top live rather well, even luxuriously in some cases. The foot soldiers receive training and subsistence. Terrorism, you see, has become a big business.

Stern's research covered a period of at least five years, during which she held positions at various prestigious institutions and achieved expertise on terrorism issues. At present, she lectures on the subject at Harvard.

Her insights, which at one time were original, have become part of the public consciousness regarding terrorists. She learned, for example, why suicide bombers flourished. They are, simply put, cheap. A suicide bomber needs little training, little support. He does not require years of being steeped in religious thought to develop the zeal for his mission. He needs only a moment of courage to wreak havoc.

Of greater value, perhaps, is her insight into the system of *madrassahs*, the religious schools that flourish throughout Islam. These schools – an estimated 48,000 of them in Pakistan alone – teach young boys the Quran and very little else. Math, science and literature – which flourished under the Golden Age of Islam a thousand years ago – are eliminated.

Stern asks a fifth-grader what he wants to be when he grows up. He wants to be a *mujahideen* and kill non-Muslims. She then asks what he thinks of America. "Down with America" is his answer. She asks why he feels that way. "Everyone says that." Do you know why? Stern presses. He answers, "No."

The biggest threats to the survival of militant Islamist groups, Stern argues, are free secular education, a rise in the literacy rate and a higher standard of living for the poor. Depriving a society of these keeps such groups well supplied with recruits.

Alan Wolfe, author of *The Transformation of American Religion*, says that the best thing we have done is to treat our war on terror as a war against terrorist groups and not as a holy war against Islam. He also thinks the tradition of American religion is one of change and innovation. Nothing could be further, Wolfe says, from the tenets of Islam as practiced by terrorists.

Stern's book illuminates this divide. Yet I found many things lacking in matters of style and choice in the writing. The chapters are introduced with lecture-like summaries and declarations, which makes the tone seem pedagogical.

Stern has admitted she wanted to write a purely academic book that would be published by a university press. Instead, her editor persuaded her to include narratives of her interviews with terrorists, and not bury them in footnotes as she had planned. A good move, except Stern is not really a storyteller. She carefully doles out information of her personal experiences, but the reader often is left wondering about colorful but incomplete details, and what else was going on.

A glossary would have been helpful. She lists so many *jihadi* groups and intelligence organizations it would have provided an easy reference point. Also, I found her diction awkward in crucial places.

Frequently, when describing her encounters with terrorist subjects, she uses past and present tense and first and third person voices indiscriminately, sometimes all in one paragraph. This is difficult, particularly so because she does not present her material on any sort of timeline. It is not clear in what order she met various people and how she formed her opinions.

Here is a real nitpick: She mentions Harvard – a lot.

These shortcomings aside, I highly recommend this work. Stern was able to wiggle herself into contact with people who are uncommon to know. She was the first American woman some of her subjects had ever seen. Her experiences are valuable to contemplate. Also of value is her final chapter, in which she talks about terrorism as a virus and offers some policy recommendations that might or might not be useful but are based on solid research and personal observation.

Stern makes the point that she is not a reporter, yet I could not help thinking of The Wall Street Journal's Daniel Pearl and his horrible death while trying to contact the very type of person she is interviewing. The same dangers attended her meetings.

Since 9/11, we have been forced to focus on what extreme beliefs can produce in human beings. Jessica Stern's book helps to clarify that process. I admire her courage and am grateful for the information she has provided.

(*Terror in the Name of God: Why Religious Militants Kill* by Jessica Stern. Ecco, 2003. 400 pages)

Steve Martin is a 'Pleasure'
October 28, 2003

Several years ago, Steve Martin wrote a brief, humorous piece for The New Yorker titled "Writing is Easy!" I read it aloud to a group of writers; we chortled and groaned over his opening: "Writing is the most easy, pain-free and happy way to pass the time of all the arts."

As everyone knows, writing is the most tortured of all the arts, practiced alone and frequently with only a bottle, a handful of pills and a stack of rejection letters for companionship.

Yet perhaps not. Steve Martin navigates an interesting and varied creative field – making a film here, writing a play or novel there, adding to his art collection or hosting discussions and award programs – and somehow makes it all appear as effortless as he revealed in his elegant little essay. "I just look deep into the heart of the rose," he wrote, "read its story, and then write it down."

Is that all there is to it? For Martin, maybe. He has followed his charming debut novel, *Shopgirl*, with an equally diverting read, *The Pleasure of My Company*. This is not the stuff of Nobel Prize winners, but if friends ask me to recommend a good book, this is what I would suggest.

Martin's work is literate, full of engaging characters who surprise in amusing ways. In addition, he has lightened up current fiction much in the way Willa Cather did in protest of three-volume 19th century novels, which she considered "overfurnished." Unlike some current 5-pound-doorstop novels, Martin does not go on to the point of tedium. He rather leaves one wishing for more – a nice bonus.

In this latest work, Martin introduces Daniel Pecan Cambridge, a sort of geek in his early 30s who lives in Santa Monica, California. Daniel has more or less barricaded himself into a restricted life of rigid behavior patterns. He is the most obsessive-compulsive individual one could meet. It takes him an hour to walk to the local Rite-Aid because he cannot manage to step off curbs and must cross streets at opposing driveways. Daniel's "favorite feeling is symmetry," and he is only comfortable when his corners are square and defined and he can identify safe borders.

Yet he is interested in life in oblique ways. Peering down on the busy, lively street from his apartment window, he concocts an imaginary romance with a real estate agent and entertains himself with endless small dramas. Do I "think too much?" he asks himself.

It appears so. His elaborate fantasy life works perfectly – as long as he stays quiet and alone. Any real interaction with other human beings throws him into a state of panic, with funny and endearing results. One hilarious episode has him delivering a speech for winning a silly contest to be the most average person. Riding to the ceremony, he tries to keep his pants from wrinkling and his skin from sweating. I do not think I laughed so much since reading Kingsley Amis's *Lucky Jim* in college.

Daniel often drops little hints to the reader that he is insane. But a discerning reader knows better. The roots of Daniel's troubles are buried in his past, and he is straining to throw off his phobias.

Lucky for Daniel, Martin plants a couple of helpful healers in his way. Clarissa is a young student-therapist whose son Teddy bonds with Daniel. The rest of the plotline is rather fragile, so disclosing much of it would ruin the intrigue of seeing it unfold. It is enough to say that Daniel begins to find ways to extend his (personally imposed) cell walls. His talent at creating mathematical "magic squares" blossoms into an application that works for his own "quiet heart." Martin gently tugs his hero along unfamiliar paths until Daniel discovers how to replace his enduring anxieties with others he can manage.

Unfortunately, Martin employs a few creaky techniques to bring his tale of Daniel to a happy ending. There is a journey, of course, and an unexpected inheritance. An almost too-perfect girl enters the scene at just the right moment. But these are nitpicks. I think life is like that sometimes – in any event, I want it to be.

Martin's fictions are full of delightful observations and touching human insights. His work reminds me of Fred Astaire's dancing in its agility and carefree style in performance that comes from serious professionalism and hard work. He does the heavy lifting in order to give his audience enjoyment.

Several years ago, Jack Nicholson won an Academy Award for portraying an obsessive-compulsive character in "As Good As It Gets." I always considered the film to be vastly overrated and inauthentic. I never believed in Nicholson's mannered behaviors, which were played broadly for comic effect. Martin has managed to create a character who has you pulling for him and who works out his destiny in ways that, though they may seem fortuitous, ring true.

Whether intended or not, the title of Martin's book is a double entendre. It's impossible not to take pleasure in the company of the protagonist – or the author.

I think I'm in love!

(*The Pleasure of My Company* by Steve Martin. Hachette Books, 2003. 163 pages)

'Intelligence' does not always win
December 12, 2003

The military has one mission, a strapping former army colonel recently told my church's discussion group: to find the enemy and kill him. In order to do that, he said, commanders must have the best possible information and know how to use it.

The current chatter of pundits blames apparent missteps in Iraq on failures of intelligence. Investigations are raging in Congress and the CIA to discover where the breakdowns in the flow of information occurred, and why the United States went forward with seemingly incorrect intelligence on weapons of mass destruction and strength of the resistance.

That good intelligence is key to winning wars is commonplace wisdom. Nothing could be clearer or, at the same time, more complex. John Keegan, perhaps Britain's foremost authority on military history, labels this idea "fashionable" then proceeds to make a strong case for a different point of view.

Keegan thinks that intelligence – both the hard military sort of data regarding troop movements and terrain and the more nuanced sort gained through human contacts and espionage – although useful, does not necessarily bring victory. Anyone interested in the truth of such speculation would be well served by reading his book *Intelligence in War: Knowledge of the Enemy from Napoleon to Al-Qaeda*.

Citing case after case, Keegan places his readers in the midst of battle, peering through fog on a Mediterranean coast at the dawn of Trafalgar in 1798 or dragging a cumbersome wagon train up and down the Shenandoah Valley during the Civil War in 1862.

Mark Twain once said, "Nothing so focuses the mind as the prospect of being hung." Certainly, generals and admirals facing the prospect of engagement with the enemy are focused wholly on winning. Any scrap of information – even, famously, the weather report presented to Eisenhower just before D-Day – is eagerly mulled over by commanders pressing for advantage.

Keegan calls it the "gold standard" – real-time intelligence or "who knows what in sufficient time to make effective use of the news."

It is instructive and more than interesting to study how victories are achieved. Admiral Nelson, whose "range and depth of powers," according to Keegan, made him the greatest admiral who ever lived, possessed a mind that "never rested." Keegan compares his constant calculations of relative position of ships and shorelines to a master chess player in full force of intellect. Nelson "consumed" information compulsively and "sought decisions in battle" as would a great financier "poised to obliterate his competitors."

Part of the value and excitement of this work lies in that statement. Keegan's analysis and the lessons he offers may be applied to fields beyond military strategy. Who in a position of leadership or policy making does not need correct information and the guts and wisdom to use it cunningly?

Yet here is the fascinating conclusion of Keegan's book. It is not enough, he argues. In the end, intelligence – even the best – is not sufficient. Strength matters, determination is paramount, everything will be decided by the fight.

Sometimes inferior troops prevail, because they go into what Keegan calls "berserker mood," plowing forward with "mindless courage." Henry V's stunning victory against overwhelming French forces at Agincourt comes to mind. Or, sometimes, a chance bit of luck turns seeming defeat into sudden victory, such as what happened in 1942 at Midway, when in the course of mere minutes American dive-bombers sank three Japanese aircraft carriers and turned the course of the war in the Pacific.

Nelson's information on the whereabouts of Napoleon's fleet was spotty. While his four-month-long chase is a model of relentless pursuit, Nelson carried the day because he knew what to do when, at last, he found his foe. Stonewall Jackson was outmanned and outgunned by McClellan's Army of the Potomac. Jackson's secret weapon was having a superior mapmaker who could sensibly guide the Confederates to sustainable positions. As his army fought over many months, the soldiers actually gained strength and were able to march 35 miles in 16 hours – if necessary, barefoot and in the rain. And, after that, they still could stand and fight, earning every triumph.

Keegan debunks the cliché that knowledge is power. Knowledge cannot defeat an enemy unless attached to blunt force, he writes.

Keegan does not recommend fumbling around in the dark, so to speak, while making life and death decisions. Correct information will "sharpen one's gaze," but the ability to "strike sure" in a tight spot remains one's best protection. Only force finally counts.

(*Intelligence in War: Knowledge of the Enemy from Napoleon to Al-Qaeda* by John Keegan. Knopf, 2003. 387 pages)

FILM REVIEWS

Those secrets of the 'Ya-Ya Sisterhood'
June 11, 2002

There is a pivotal scene in the film "Gone With the Wind" when Scarlett O'Hara, desperate for money and weary from overwork, yanks her mother's curtains from their fixture and drapes her tired body in green velvet, defying her mammy, who stomps around the parlor lamenting the desecration of "Miss Ellen's portieres."

Scarlett flaunts her new dress in Atlanta, scrounges the needed tax money, flees the plantation drudgery and gets back into the game.

Great scene. Now try to imagine the movie without it.

In Rebecca Wells' novel *Divine Secrets of the Ya-Ya Sisterhood*, in which the main character, Vivi Walker, is sent to a convent school by her deranged mother who has gone mad with perverted piety, Vivi submits to the hatred of a cruel Mother Superior.

Her very breath is nearly extinguished by forces she does not understand until Teensy – one of her Ya-Ya sisters – and Teensy's mother, Genevieve, arrive to spring her from this adolescent concentration camp.

As they blast away in a Packard huge enough to rocket to the moon, Genevieve tells the girls: "Life is short, but it is wide. This, too, shall pass."

Here is wisdom enough for daughters who will listen and a scene dense with the complexity of powerful motherhood, of redemption through the strength of love. Every woman who read the novel drank in that scene.

The scene is not in the movie.

What could screenwriter and director Callie Khouri have been thinking? While not absolutely disastrous, the omission of Vivi's rescue makes it hard to connect the dots leading to her future collapse. If that episode was in fact filmed and is presently residing in a vault somewhere, I seriously suggest that Khouri restore it to the video version.

Now for the good part.

Vivi, Teensy, Caro and Necie (played, respectively, by Ellen Burstyn, Fionnula Flanagan, Shirley Knight and Maggie Smith) mingle their blood to create the silly yet enduring rituals of Ya-Ya sisterhood. We see them sharing laughter, music, growing pains and large beds, indulging in endless sleepovers as they stagger toward confusing adulthood and motherhood.

Then the cycle begins again with their own children – specifically with Vivi's elder daughter Siddalee, played by Sandra Bullock. Siddalee, a successful playwright, commits a daughter's greatest betrayal. She talks honestly to a reporter about her childhood and the relationship with her mother.

As a result, war breaks out. The Ya-Ya sisters kidnap Sidda to reveal the secrets that ultimately bring about reconciliation between mother and daughter. But in order to achieve this resolution, each woman must revisit a great deal of past grief, alcoholism, child abuse and mental illness.

There are men in this movie, but they mostly drink beer and keep out of the way. I am not sure what was on James Garner's mind when he accepted the role of Vivi's long-suffering husband Shep, but it was nice to see him trying to bring a semblance of order and sanity to Burstyn's overwrought tirades. (On "The Tonight Show," Jay Leno joked that the movie netted 16.4 million dollars – the .4, he said, coming from the men who watched it.)

Smith, naturally, steals every scene in her sly and sublime manner.

This sort of film follows a tried-and-true formula: Women must struggle and suffer, hurt others and be hurt in return, laugh and cry and celebrate themselves, and in this way we all learn how to get on in the world and attain the requisite forgiveness.

One goes to these films not necessarily to learn about the characters, but to learn about one's own life. Women's films are meant to serve as catalysts. In this sense, "Divine Secrets" delivers the goods.

If I wanted to quibble – and like Vivi, Sidda and the others, I sometimes do – I'd say the actress Ya-Ya mothers are about a decade too old for the story. Also, the movie fails to solve the puzzle of why these bright spunky Southern girls who grew up to marry husbands who buy them Bentleys and live in huge white houses with pillars and porches and servants bringing them Bloody Marys must inevitably become alcoholic nutcases.

Forget the small stuff. Just go. Go with a friend – or, better yet, with 10 friends. Afterward, share some food and wine and talk about your lives. Just be prepared to exchange puzzled queries, as my friends and I did at a recent screening.
Where was the convent scene?

("Divine Secrets of the Ya-Ya Sisterhood." Warner Bros. 2002. 116 minutes. PG-13)

Where was Seabiscuit?
July 25, 2003

In her marvel of a book *Seabiscuit: An American Legend*, it takes Laura Hillenbrand a brisk 30 pages to sketch in the backgrounds of the three principal human characters before the star – the runty-but-game horse of the title – enters the scene.

In the film "Seabiscuit," writer-director Gary Ross makes the audience wait 50 long minutes, the screenwriting equivalent of 50 pages – an eternity – for the fabled horse to make his appearance. Even then, he is relegated to background status.

Though the personal stories of Charles Howard, the owner; Tom Smith, the trainer, and Red Pollard, the jockey, are compelling – as written by Hillenbrand – somehow on the screen they become confusing and tiresome.

When the source material for a film is well-known to an audience, certain expectations accompany patrons into the theater. Yet surely even a person who knows nothing about this remarkable animal and his place in American history might be let down here to mutter, as I did leaving a recent screening, "Where was the horse?"

Inexplicably, the film begins with the dignified voice of historian David McCullough, telling us about the Model T and Henry Ford's desire to produce an affordable car for the common man. Faded period photographs accompany McCullough's narrative insertions, similar to the style of documentary filmmaker Ken Burns. This technique lends a stately importance to the story, but it quickly becomes annoying and seems to slow the action in what is, after all, a moving picture.

The oddest example in this regard is the director's choice in the big scene – the renowned match race between Seabiscuit and Triple Crown winner War Admiral. We have heard Tom Smith (played by Chris Cooper) say that the horse who breaks first will most likely win the race, and we have seen him train little Seabiscuit to jump at the sound of a fire alarm. We see the starter's finger poised over the button that will ring the bell and then ... and then ... the director cuts to photos of people sitting around their radios in homes and cars, listening to the broadcast. Unbelievable, but he never shows the beginning of the race!

These are just technicalities. The real disappointment of "Seabiscuit" is we never really get to "see" the horse. Quick cuts show bits and pieces, mostly at a distance, but the lingering shots that would be necessary to illuminate his legendary eyes and unusual body language are not there.

Hillenbrand, in her elegant prose, described an animal with immense personality who fairly danced off the page. As a colt, Seabiscuit was ignored and ill-used for several years, until a gifted trainer actually made eye-contact and perceived the intelligence and spirit within his inauspicious exterior. But it was Charles Howard, a man of substantial wealth and charisma, who instantly fell in love with this unpromising thoroughbred and possessed the money, patience and faith to make him a champion.

It's that exceptional champion's quality Hillenbrand so carefully revealed, how a winning horse will swagger and even intimidate competitors. Seabiscuit earned his fame through his winning heart, craving victory so much his jockey said of him, "You could kill him before he'd quit."

Ross fails to portray this wonderful intimacy with the horse on screen. Instead, we have Howard (Jeff Bridges), Smith and Pollard (Tobey Maguire) skulking around Pimlico Race Course in a mock James Bond caper to spy on arch rival War Admiral. Such hokey nonsense! Instead of getting into the soul of this icon, we follow the biographies of three men and try to make sense of their lives.

Yet their true histories are muddled or downright fabricated in pointless ways. Why not show, for instance, the colorful way Howard, a car salesman, began to amass his fortune? He drove his entire inventory – three Buicks he'd been unable to sell – into the aftermath of the San Francisco earthquake of 1906 and used them as ambulances or supply wagons. A few years later, he owned dealerships all over the West.

Also, the movie suggests the whole country was rooting for Seabiscuit in the match race, but 95 percent of the gate had bet against him. And why not take a few seconds to portray President Roosevelt keeping a roomful of advisers waiting in the White House while he listened to the race call?

Hillenbrand suffers from a debilitating illness. Barely able to move physically, she wrote her book in a cramped room, her imagination immersed in the world of horses and racing. Through words alone, she created the sense of being seated on a horse and driving the half-ton beast at lickety-split speed around a muddy, uncertain track.

The best the film offers are many, many shots looking at mounted jockeys' rear ends. Fancy mechanical horses were used for close-ups in order to show the jockeys talking to one another during a race, and this inauthenticity speaks loudly.

Even more mechanical are the repetitive lines of tepid dialogue and – over and over – facial reaction shots expressing anxiety and tension before and during races. Overworked in this regard are the actors playing Howard's wife, Marcela (Valerie Mahaffey), and faithful old groom, Sam (Kingston DuCoeur). Saying little, their worried brows furrow time and again.

Hillenbrand pushes her narrative along, going deeper into the sport of racing but never letting go of her subject and never forgetting she is writing a love story.

The most egregious omission from the film is perhaps the failure to depict the years of Seabiscuit's retirement. Ross chooses to fade out before the champion finishes his last race. Not to include an epilogue showing Howard's singular devotion beyond the natural life of his beloved horse defies understanding. Even a written coda would have been better.

A film is not a book, and each director enjoys vast creative license. But in this case, the book is about something specific. It's about Seabiscuit.

I don't know what this film is about, but it's not about that horse. It might be about the Great Depression or something called "the beginning and end of imagination." It is sort of about open plains and mountains versus industry. There's a lot of jabber about "the little guy." Maybe it's about him. Many scenes – lively ones at that – depict how to create sound effects for radio. Is it about what the character called Howard keeps saying, "The future is the finish line?"

Darned if I know. Take your pick. The unfortunate thing is, something precious was handed to Ross on a platter, which he has dropped. Nothing disappoints like wasted opportunity.

Although it is sad that Hillenbrand got cheated out of a great film version of her work, the real sorrow lies elsewhere.

Seabiscuit, old buddy, you deserve better.

("Seabiscuit." Universal. 2003. 140 minutes. PG-13)

'Sun' goes under a cloud
October 6, 2003

Some years ago, my book group – along with thousands of others – read and discussed *Under the Tuscan Sun*, a memoir by Frances Mayes, an author totally unknown to us. Her unfamiliarity was short-lived. Mayes came alive and became almost a personal friend as she described her experience of purchasing, renovating and living in Bramasole, a decrepit Tuscan farmhouse that became a loving work-in-progress. As she and her partner and later-to-be husband Ed hammer nails, dig in their orchard and interact with the local citizens, a marvelous tale unfolds about discovering a new culture, of food and energetic fun.

Sun is a well-told, engaging story, and every woman I know who read the book fantasized herself as its heroine and dreamed of going to Tuscany, finding a house, et cetera.

Now comes a film of the same title, written and directed by Audrey Wells. I had eagerly been looking forward to seeing it, but I began to have a bad feeling when the distributors ran a number of sneak previews. It's usually not a good sign. It means the producers are trying to build good word of mouth before the reviews come out.

My intuition was correct. Warning to book clubs: This screen adaptation will insult your intelligence. The usual disclaimer should be turned around to read: The names in this movie are real; everything else has been changed.

Oh, yes, there is a character called Frances Mayes and a house called Bramasole, but as for the rest – where to begin?

Not that the situation is unusual. It is common for Hollywood to buy up non-fiction books of mass popular appeal and whip up some totally unrelated fictional story, retaining only the best-selling title. Remember *Sex and the Single Girl*? That book was a rather dry compendium of statistics and anecdotal research. Yet it created the excuse for re-inventing Helen Gurley Brown as a ditsy psychologist embodied by Natalie Wood. *Sun*, the book, has a commanding heroine with an authentic narrative voice and a lot more going for it. Somehow, during the transfer to screen, all that has been tossed into the dumpster.

We meet the movie Frances, a college professor, writer and book reviewer who is in the process of a humiliating divorce. Persuaded by an oily lawyer, she voluntarily gives up her own spectacular house in San Francisco to her unfaithful husband and his pregnant girlfriend. Taking nothing but three cartons of books, she just walks away from her gorgeous furniture and moves into the crummiest, most dispiriting short-term rental seen on screen since Ralph and Alice Kramden's apartment in "The Honeymooners."

I found that set-up to be improbable, even laughable. Nothing that followed changed my mind. Diane Lane as the movie Frances is great-looking and somewhat younger than Mayes was when she began her sojourn in Tuscany. She is unattached romantically, unlike the real woman. That part is okay; her situation presents many possibilities for drama, and I'm all for exercising intelligent poetic license. The problem is, as written, the scenes are so ... lame, and they seem to take forever to play out. I lost interest, so many times, just waiting for something to happen.

It isn't Lane's fault, but her lines are boring. Instead of a main character who has enough gumption to pursue a decades-old attraction to Tuscan culture, Lane, who seems never even to have heard of a country called Italy, is given a trip there by two lesbian friends. She literally jumps off a tour bus to fall into a For Sale sign. Then, instead of possessing the fortitude to deal with the inexplicable intricacies of Italian real estate while taking precarious financial risk, the movie Frances simply attracts an agent who seems able to cut through all the bureaucratic red tape in mere seconds. And though happily married, he shows up at all hours to solve her domestic traumas, such how to find the snake hiding in the kitchen. How fortunate. He never has anything better to do than listen to her emotional problems.

All the men she meets are like that, appearing at all-too-convenient moments, getting her out of jams and helping her a few kilometers further along the path toward renewed self-esteem and feeling good about herself again. In other words, the film is about what Hollywood thinks women want to see. It's not worth anyone's time for me to recount the plot. Trust me, you've seen this one before, many times.

You've also heard it. During the course of the film, lines are repeated, over and over. Like the one that states, "Terrible ideas are the best ones," or "They built the tracks from Vienna to Venice before they had a train to ride them." Stuff like that. Every point or nuance is driven home with a sledge hammer. Every character speaks philosophically, teaching the teacher about life, telling her repeatedly not to be so sad, that regrets "are a waste of time," and that she cannot keep "wallowing."

She rises out of her depression long enough to pick up a guy on the streets of Rome and immediately scamper off with him to the Amalfi coast. Wow! No wallowing there. After a night of passion, which she later describes euphemistically as "ladybugs" – don't ask – her Italian stallion says, soulfully, "If you smash into something good, you should hold on until it's time to let go." Naturally, a few frames later, that time arrives. At one point, she sobs that she wants cooking, a baby and a wedding in her house. Surprise, surprise! That, too, comes to pass. It's the way this film goes. It announces itself, repeats itself and then draws every conclusion for you with a giant red marker.

There is too much tell and not enough show. The real Frances discovered Tuscany, yet Lane discovers only herself. Aside from a few grainy hillside shots and some market moments, there is not much of Tuscany – certainly nothing like the sense of place that drenched "A Room With a View" or Kenneth Branagh's ravishing version of Shakespeare's "Much Ado About Nothing." If there's going to be an absence of engrossing drama, at least give us a decent travelogue.

Writer/director Wells gave an interview to "Fresh Air" host Terry Gross on NPR, in which she told how she once faked her way into a job as a disc jockey for a radio station in San Francisco. The station manager asked her to list the top 100 jazz albums. Knowing absolutely nothing about jazz, Wells went to the station library and found the albums with the most worn covers and listed those. She got the job.

Some of that MO seems to have survived as she tries to fake her way through this movie. She keeps throwing in shopworn scenes and bits of plot from great films. It is Italy, after all, so there is the obligatory Romeo and Juliet couple whom Frances champions. In a supporting role, Lindsay Duncan plays Katherine, a fading 40-ish actress and free lover who keeps spouting favorite maxims from her beloved "Federico" – Fellini, that is – who told her, "Always keep your childish innocence."

Katherine loses it temporarily one evening and, despondent over the loss of her young lover, plays out the Anita Ekberg scene in "La Dolce Vita," dancing in a fountain in a strapless black gown. Later, she rallies to become Scarlett O'Hara at the barbecue, surrounded by adoring beaux. Katherine and Frances share a tender moment of recalling the influence of Fellini's "The Nights of Cabiria." By my calculations, these two gals were exactly age zero when the master was at the peak of his career. All this gabble is meaningless torture. Since Lane has barely heard about Italy, how is she so acquainted with the work of this famous – but definitely outdated – director?

Somehow, without Lane's having any apparent means of financial support, the house comes together, but the picture never does. Frances Mayes, the real one, is on record as praising this film, saying how much pleasure she has derived from seeing her story portrayed. I do not blame her. Two books followed *Under the Tuscan Sun*: *Bella Tuscany* and *In Tuscany*. Also, I've seen articles about a tie-in line of furniture. She has a lot at stake with her one-woman Tuscan cottage industry, so it's not unexpected she'd try to promote the heck out of the film.

I just pray it does not become too big a hit, because if so, someone might take a meeting and come up with the bright idea of pitching Audrey Wells as the writer/director of *The Lovely Bones* or *The Da Vinci Code*. I shudder to think. Perhaps a better fit would be for her to fashion a smash fictional movie out of *The South Beach Diet* or, better yet, *Living History*.

("Under the Tuscan Sun." Touchstone Pictures. 113 minutes. PG-13)

'Sylvia' alive on screen
November 4, 2003

There is simply no way to condense the complexity and drama of the seven-year Sylvia Plath-Ted Hughes marriage into a scant two-hour movie. Yet director Christine Jeffs and writer John Brownlow manage to get a story onto the screen that is alive, engrossing and does not demean the memories of its subjects. In other words, "Sylvia" is a minor triumph.

Sylvia Plath's suicide at the age of 30 during a bleak February in London in 1963 has left generations of women shivering with empathic rage, vowing revenge against the husband they branded – immediately – as the culprit and cause of her death. His famous infidelity and lack of attention to her art have become legend among feminists and Sylvia wannabes, who have fed off stories of her tortured, fragile soul.

Poor Ted Hughes. He did not have a chance against the legions of women warriors who have assaulted him, and his memory, for 40 years. He realized almost instantly what he was up against and maintained an elegant silence against his critics until a few months before his death in 1999, when he published his own version of his relationship with Sylvia in a book of poems titled *Birthday Letters*.

Given the heat of the factions warring over Sylvia's bones during the past decades, I find it remarkable that the film presents such a balanced view of these two poets and their tragic marriage. I know Plath devotees will pick over every scene and nuance, and they will find much information either missing in this saga or somehow misconstrued. Perhaps the filmmakers allowed themselves too great a poetic license, playing around needlessly, it seems, with the timeline and other inexplicable changes of fact.

Sylvia's mother, for example, attended her daughter's wedding to Ted, a brief four months after the couple met at a raucous party at Cambridge University, where Ted ripped off her scarf and an earring to keep as "trophies." The film has Aurelia Plath (played by Blythe Danner) meeting her son-in-law in the United States and frigidly hosting a party for the newlyweds, all the while expressing disapproval, saying only that he is "different" and doubting that he will be able to support Sylvia.

Yet Hughes wrote achingly of his wedding day, with his bride in her "pink wool knitted dress ... so slender and new and naked, a nodding spray of wet lilac." He described her mother as "brave even in this U.S. Foreign Affairs gamble, (who) acted all bridesmaids and all guests, even ... represented my family who had heard nothing about it." And Aurelia gave them the gift of a cottage on Cape Cod for a summer so they could write and enjoy a honeymoon.

Sometimes truth does not provide conflict enough.

The film also conveys the impression that the young marrieds lived in dank places, and Sylvia suffered writer's block for the entire seven years of their union while Ted soared in fame and popularity. Again, not close to reality. They spent a lot of time fixing up their various abodes, and Ted generally was helpful about sharing household duties.

The thing was, it was the '50s, after all. Sylvia's dream of becoming a great poet was linked closely with her other dreams of living in a grand house, having darling children and cooking passionately for a man to prove her goodness. She did not understand all those lovely dreams might clash when tested. She was a perfectionist and demanded the best of herself. Somehow, she did manage to produce two children, a novel and a published book of poetry, all the while teaching, moving to at least five different homes and promoting Ted's career. Not bad for a woman who probably suffered from bipolar disorder.

The film displays beautifully, through visual and aural imagery, the sensory life of poets – quite an accomplishment. Every scene seems bathed in the wet mucus of creation. Walls are painted in dark shiny gloss, and water drenches the landscapes. Birds' wings flutter in frustration or exaltation; a subtle but bitter wind alters the mood of lovemaking. Slight gestures and facial expressions condense into tiny moments of distilled intensity, as when a poem is burned to its essence and every carefully chosen word combines to complete the meaning.

Ted and Sylvia are in a rowboat; she tells him, "I'm all dried up." He has taken a walk that morning and a poem burst in his head and spilled over onto the page. "It's no secret," he responds. "You pick a subject and stick your head into it." She demurs, "I don't have a subject." He blunders, she resists, and so together absorbed, they drift out to sea, but not of their own volition. "Tide's dragging us out," Ted mutters. "People drown like this."

This is just about perfect, and it feels correct even if it never happened.

I expected the film to be more "talky" and contain endless passages of recited poetry. What a pleasant surprise to find it such a visual delight and the poetry more like musical accompaniment. Of course, it must include scenes of mental disintegration, and the ending is wrenching to watch unfold. But when the medics come to take Sylvia away, her lifeless body, carried out through the snow, is wrapped in a scarlet blanket. Years later, Hughes wrote, "Red was your color ... you reveled in red."

Hughes came to know Plath more deeply after her death through reading her journals, discovering then "the shock of your joy."

Her journals are a revelation, after reading only the poetry. How alive she was, and how mercurial her moods. She put down every little mood swing and desire. In her private writing, Plath gives evidence of being what my mother's generation called "oversexed," generously smearing her lips with bright crimson. She liked boys, and they seemed to like her. Yet she did not stray from the marriage, while Hughes certainly did. He left her a few months before her suicide. Then, adding to the tragedy – and not mentioned in the movie – six years later, the woman for whom he left Sylvia committed suicide in the same manner, taking their four-year-old daughter with her.

"Sylvia" is not the final word on the Plath-Hughes marriage. Their story will continue to fascinate new generations. New source materials are just now being released from an archive at Emory University in Atlanta. Yet I think, for now, this film will stand on its own as a vivid and plausible record. It has a rare quality of integrity, in large part because of the performances of Gwyneth Paltrow (Danner's real-life daughter) and Daniel Craig as Sylvia and Ted. They are just magnificent.

Craig, although looking older than Hughes' age of 25 when they met, embodies the hulking, primal poet at his devastating peak of attractiveness. Paltrow – of the chiseled, porcelain features – manages to capture Plath's strangely shapeless and transitory face, which her friends called "rubbery." Ted later wrote that face "made every camera your enemy."

I remember reading years ago that a director once told Spencer Tracy to let his stubble grow for a scene. Tracy refused, saying, "I'll act unshaven." In "Sylvia," Paltrow "acts" liquid; I've never seen her more expressive or using her unique force so powerfully.

Both Ted and Sylvia must have been tough to live with at times. It's good to see him treated fairly; at least one new book will explore his side of the partnership. Yet I think these two have taken many secrets with them, and might, like Heathcliff and Cathy, be joined in death to wander over their own unquiet graves and leave the rest of us to wonder.

("Sylvia." BBC Pictures. 100 minutes. R)

COMMENTARY

The National Book Festival: Literacy revived
October 15, 2002

As a former literacy tutor, it is alarming to contemplate that more than a third of American adults do not read well enough to fill out a job application or help their children with homework.

Functional literacy is on the decline in our country. Perhaps of even greater concern is the growing problem of aliteracy, referring to those who can read but do not.

Librarians tell us reading is in trouble. Their students choose movies, music, Web surfing – any leisure activity except curling up with a book. Yet, in our present atmosphere of fear and insecurity because of the charged geopolitical crisis, polls indicate people are snatching up books, groping for meaning through the written word.

First Lady Laura Bush recently addressed this apparent contradictory trend, saying, "We've needed the comfort of good books to read and families to read with."

On Saturday these ideas took shape on the West Lawn of the Capitol in Washington, D.C., where the Library of Congress and the first lady hosted the National Book Festival, the second of what is to be an annual adventure designed to promote the fun of reading.

For seven hours, dozens of American authors, illustrators, actors and musicians enlightened and entertained crowds under the vast canopies of festive tents labeled Fiction and Imagination,

Mystery and Thrillers, History and Biography or Children and Young Adult. Within short strolling distance, it was possible to sample the very best writers and storytellers in America. Every half-hour, the programs changed, and though it was impossible to attend every reading or discussion, the quantity of choice and degree of excellence astounded.

Most of the writers spoke to overflow crowds, even though the tents accommodated 200 to 300 seated patrons. The superb audio systems were a pleasant surprise, reaching to the outer edges of each audience.

You could not go wrong. Billy Collins, our Poet Laureate, was his usual delightful self, amusing the audience with a poem based on the fact that it took the skins of 300 sheep to produce one Gutenberg Bible. Tim O'Brien, holding forth in a suit and his signature baseball cap, read in a tough and aggressive voice what he called "a gorgeous piece of writing" from his new novel, *July, July*. Tony Hillerman had them standing 10 deep on all sides as he spun out colorful tales about Taos, New Mexico.

Mrs. Bush watched the Georgia Sea Island Singers tell stories and sing about plantation heritage. She tapped out a gentle hambone rhythm along with other listeners and signed programs for a few shy children. Thunderous applause frequently broke out and rolled across the lawn.

Down by the reflecting pool, food pavilions served delicious ethnic dishes for modest prices. Everything else at the festival was free. Children lined up at the Reading Is Fundamental booth to receive free books. At the Pavilion of States, representatives from each state passed out information about local authors and so many freebies – maps, colorful posters, pencils, book marks – that people staggered under the weight of their collections.

Live bands featuring Dixieland, jazz and Cajun music played constantly for the crowds. All the authors spent time signing books for their fans, the lines meandering across the Mall seemed to replenish themselves all afternoon.

Wherever you looked were smiling engaged adults and happy enthusiastic children. Even in late afternoon, the tents stayed at capacity. Christopher Buckley had them rolling in the aisles, and Mary and Carol Higgins Clark were packing them in until well after 4 p.m. James McPherson. David McCullough. So many authors, so little time.

You would have thought reading was as popular as basketball. On that note, Jerry Stackhouse and Jahidi White of the NBA, and Swin Cash and Stacey Dales-Schuman of the WNBA showed up to promote to young adults the necessity of learning to read.

Does this event move the ball forward in the solution of our literacy problems? It might be impossible to gauge for a while. Judging by the enthusiasm and spirit present, however, it cannot hurt and must give hope to hard-working librarians everywhere.

As a veteran attendee of literary readings, I thought about what made this day so different from the usual book tour to promote authors. Typically, a writer flies into town and runs from radio show to classroom, ending up that evening in a dreary corner of a book store to read and talk to a few fans who are likewise tired but dogged.

I cannot overstate the zesty energy emanating from the authors at this festival. One especially caught the mood for me: Henry Louis Gates, Jr., head of the Afro-American Studies program at Harvard University, among other things. Lively and literate, he thanked Laura Bush and then made humorous comments about being a "Demma ... Demma..."

Gates's presentation centered on discovering an original manuscript by a slave woman and his subsequent editing and publishing of her story. The audience was huge, some people even sitting on slightly muddy turf. As Gates finished to prolonged applause, an African-American woman sitting behind me said, "He makes smart cool!"

Later, I heard an interview Gates did on C-SPAN. Asked if he was surprised to be invited to the festival, given that his politics are so different from the administration, he answered that he enjoyed going to the White House and found the first lady to be an intelligent and informed woman. And then he said something amazing. "I don't know what Laura Bush's politics are." What an elegant, hope-reviving statement!

Gates expressed the very essence of this event. In this partisan-obsessed town, the National Book Festival is not about politics or dividing along lines of ideology but rather about gathering and sharing and reading and joy.

Smart is cool, indeed.

Books for Baghdad
April 9, 2003

When I was around eight years old, my mother gave me a bookmark with these words printed on it: "Whenever I get a little money, I buy books. If I have any left over, I buy food and clothing."

That concept stitched itself into my brain, forming a lifelong perception of values and what we consider to be necessities. In a way, that quotation gave me permission to indulge my passion for acquiring books, to spend thousands of unapologetic hours browsing book stores and libraries – sometimes purposefully and sometimes idly – touching, scanning and leafing through books.

I especially love to read about the subject of books and reading. Recently, I reviewed *The Hemingway Book Club of Kosovo*, Paula Huntley's journal recounting her experience teaching English to a group of young post-war Albanians. These students all had suffered deprivation and loss, fear and near-death as they fled to refugee camps while their homes and possessions burned. Having barely survived hideous atrocities, they nevertheless eagerly attended Huntley's class, embracing the study of literature as a way to go forward and begin living again.

The father of one bright pupil was particularly affecting. He wanted to know all about the size of American universities and how many books are in the libraries. "My father would like to see sometime a library with many books," Leonard, the student, told his teacher.

As one who constantly plans which of my precious books I would grab if my house were to catch fire, I read the account of that war with palpable pain. I recall similar emotion when, back in the 1960s, I watched Francois Truffaut's "Fahrenheit 451." Based on Ray Bradbury's futuristic novel, the film depicts a world where squads of goon-like firemen break into people's houses and burn their books. Under this totalitarian regime, literature is considered too connected to freedom, and eliminating books is therefore a means of controlling the population.

One especially grisly scene shows a pile of books burning as a gang of disciplined thugs heaps more and more on the pyre, pages scorching then slowly curling, titles dissolving, paper disintegrating into upward drifting ash – Austen, Salinger, Tolstoy, Brontë. I became almost nauseated watching. It was my idea of a horror movie.

How to live without books? What if circumstances forced this unimaginable fate on you?

War and tyranny are such circumstances.

One benefit – if I may call it that – of war is its power to focus rapt attention on a specific country, providing the world with abbreviated lessons in geography and history. My personal current crash course in this regard has led to a fascination with the Iraqi people and their rich culture and civilization stretching back nearly seven millennia.

In my imagination, Baghdad was always the city of Aladdin's lamp and exotic architecture, of *A Thousand and One Nights*. I was vaguely aware that at one time Baghdad existed as the cultural center of the whole world. Yet not until I read an article by Rajiv Chandrasekaran in the March 10 Washington Post did I understand the depth of intellect in this proud and majestic capital city.

In the 9th century, the benevolent leaders of Baghdad, known as caliphs, built a great library called the House of Wisdom. This absolute jewel, home to the finest scholars of mathematics and translators of literature, illuminated all of Islam until invading Mongols destroyed its contents in the 13th century. The books and precious manuscripts were either burned or dumped into the Tigris River.

That such an unspeakable and ignominious deed did not destroy the people's almost romantic attachment to their books is remarkable. Through the centuries, this cultured populace earned a reputation expressed in this statement Chandrasekaran quotes from the Arabic: "Cairo writes, Beirut publishes, Baghdad reads."

As recently as the 1970s, bookstores and art galleries flourished in this vibrant city. But today, after decades of war, sanctions, repression and despotic government, citizens have few books, seeking them rather hopelessly in vestiges of once-thriving marketplaces. A little shop named House of Wisdom used to carry books but now only offers stationery. Most people have been forced to sell off their personal libraries just to survive.

The other day, as I watched on TV the ships delivering food and water and medicine for hungry and thirsty people, I began to dream about other forms of humanitarian aid – nourishment for famished intellects and starved minds. Just as books became a means of recovery for those students in Kosovo, surely the people of Iraq deserve no less. What joy to see a new type of relief worker, handing bright volumes into eager hands. Wouldn't it be thrilling to see a great ship sail into port laden with materials to build a modern House of Wisdom and crates of books to fill its shelves?

Hasn't this parched and patient nation earned a glistening new library as an ornament attesting to their new liberty? How can we not come together and give these people a tiny bit of glory from their past as a way to celebrate hope for the future?

As a firm believer in beauty and knowledge as enduring forms of solace, I therefore put forth a modest proposal for an exquisite free library system for Iraq. I envision a system based on the one developed by that famous immigrant to America, Andrew Carnegie: a network of main libraries spawning branches until every community, no matter how small, enjoys its own treasure trove of books.

But first, a magnificent main library must be erected in Baghdad, glistening and even a bit ostentatious, smack dab in the center of a tyrant's former seat of power. What better use for Saddam's main palace, sitting on prime riverfront real estate and recently having become available?

If I had my way, the United States and other willing nations and sponsors would form a new coalition whose purpose it is to provide this gift, a fitting tribute symbolizing a return to civility in Iraq. I call on all who share my passion for books to consider this matter and lend support. Most likely this will require years of dedicated effort.

But what rewards!

Let us begin!

A fond new gaze at Anne Frank
August 6, 2003

The camera loved her.

A series of school photos, taken from 1935 to 1942 when she grew from six to 13 years old, shows a lively face framed with fly-away hair, a charming overbite and dark, ink-pot eyes.

In one of her diary entries, she joked about going to "Hollywood" and becoming a screen star. She plastered a wall in the Secret Annex with pictures of her movie heroines, but Anne Frank became a different sort of idol.

The United States Holocaust Memorial Museum in Washington, D.C., is presently hosting an exhibit that, although it includes marvelous vintage photographs, focuses on Anne Frank, the writer. So much has been written about Anne, it is wonderful to see gathered artifacts that remind us of her art, practiced through the simple act of recording her thoughts in a diary.

On the day I visited there recently, crowds shuffled through the dim rooms in respectful near-silence. It seemed no one wished to despoil the hushed atmosphere.

Anne Frank has come to symbolize the undaunted spirit of Holocaust survival – even though she died at age 15, a few weeks before the Allies liberated the Bergen-Belsen camp where she was sent with her sister Margot. Anne wrote perhaps her most famous passage – "I still believe, in spite of everything, that people are truly good at heart." – one month before troops raided her family's hiding place in Amsterdam and captured everyone in the household.

No matter how many times I read *The Diary of a Young Girl* or hear her story, I always hope for a different ending, for the Americans to get there sooner, for this girl on the cusp of womanhood to live and have her chance at a long, full life.

I visited the exhibit hoping to see the diary itself. A facsimile rests under glass together with reproduced pages. It is more than satisfying. I studied each scrap.

The red-plaid diary was a gift for her 13th birthday. She instantly turned to its blank pages for support and comfort, naming it "Kitty" and jotting down that she wanted the book to be a "true friend." It was the first thing she packed when her family was forced to move from their home. "Memories mean more to me than dresses," she wrote.

From the first page, the diary evoked from her the confiding tone. She did not know she was writing for a future audience of millions of readers. So intimate is Anne's style that each reader feels kinship and a personal connection. I have heard this sentiment repeated countless times.

Although she fretted on paper, wondering whether she possessed "real talent," there is no doubt she was, truly, a writer. She pounced on words as if they were flowers waiting to be gathered, scratching on everything, captioning the photos in her album, commenting on what she was thinking about or doing in the pictures.

The photos break your heart in their depiction of everyday, joyous family life. Two sisters at the beach, eating dripping ice cream cones. School friends playing with hoops and scooters. Aunties and grannies relaxing in summer gardens.

The early pages of her diary preserve her childish and uneven handwriting. She pasted in pictures of herself and scrawled humorous subheads and titles, in essence saying, "Look at me!" Later, when she begins to copy over her work – possibly for future publication – her hand is sure, her pages are carefully numbered and her observations mature into literate, deeper thoughts. Some of the original pages presented here appear with a riveting inkblot or two, a few crossed-out phrases and interesting smudges.

As I wandered through the exhibit, I watched a girl, eight years old or so and wearing lipstick and nail polish, press on a glass case, unconsciously moving closer to the very touch of this writer. The guard told her, gently, to stand back. I understand her yearning. Many of us crave the tactile sense of original manuscripts. The pages represent the very soul of this unusual/ordinary adolescent; the diary was the lifeline she clung to through unimaginable horror. "I can shake off everything if I write," Anne tells us. "My sorrows disappear; my courage is reborn."

Anne scribbled away during her two years in the Secret Annex - her refuge from Nazi terror – composing fairy tales, short stories, essays and even the beginnings of a novel. She called these works, several of which are displayed in the museum, her "pen-children." Adopting the habit of many famous writers, she collected favorite quotations in a volume she titled "Book of Nice Sentences."

She wrestled with herself on the page, crying out, "I'm split in two." Her "better and finer side" battled with her "light hearted and chatterbox side." She was always afraid to show "all kinds of things that lie buried deep in my heart." She tried out different techniques and styles, documenting the quarrels of her fellow exiles, fashioning small dramas from arguments over dishes.

By any standard, not even considering her circumstances, her output was prodigious. Writing became her necessity.

In a videotaped interview included in the exhibit, Miep Gies, the faithful employee of Anne's father who supplied the family with food, books and news from the outside, describes a moment when she interrupted Anne at her writing desk. The girl looked up, with an "expression of pent-up fury," reports Gies. When she wrote, she let it pour out of her – curiosity, frustration, anger, sorrow and exaltation. At her young age, she discovered what it was to be a working writer.

It's a good thing wise heads protect her precious, immortal pages, else they would be shredded by the sheer force of love by her devoted admirers. Lucky for the world, we can reproduce her words and endlessly share their insights.

Here is my favorite passage:

> *I don't have much in the way of money or worldly possessions, I'm not beautiful, intelligent or clever, but I'm happy, and I intend to stay that way! I was born happy, I love people, I have a trusting nature, and I'd like everyone else to be happy too.*

A nice surprise among the treasures in the exhibit is a 14-second film, the only known footage of Anne. It was taken in 1941 when she was 12 years old. She is standing on a balcony, watching a wedding scene down in the street. She looks over and sees the camera pointed at her. She looks up to the sky, then into the apartment behind her, calling to someone inside. She looks back at the camera, poses a bit, then loses interest and directs her attention once again to the action in the street.

I watched this tiny but vivid film – a wisp – a dozen times. The image captures Anne as she wished herself, and everyone, to be: happy. I don't know why, but I'm absurdly pleased that she turns away from the camera and goes back to studying whatever is going on below her stone balcony. Her fascination with looking out at life and observing its action and drama, coupled with her powers of self-reflection and the courage to look deeply within her own heart, would have served her well had she been granted the time to mature as a writer.

The museum has extended the exhibit through December. It is not enough time for all the new generations who yet need to meet Anne and her humble diary. There never will be enough time.

Dedicated to the ones she loves
September 2, 2003

Hillary Clinton dedicated her book to me!
　　Imagine how thrilled I was to open *Living History* and read:
　　　　To my parents,
　　　　my husband,
　　　　my daughter –
　　　　and all the good souls around the world
　　　　whose inspiration, prayers, support and love
　　　　blessed my heart and sustained me in
　　　　the years of living history.
Yep, that's me – one of the "good souls." I remember pushing my way to the front of a crowd gathered by the Reflecting Pool in the winter of 1993, straining to get a glimpse of the new first-couple-to-be, while celebrities serenaded their inaugural. I must admit, Aretha Franklin belting out "R-E-S-P-E-C-T" equally drew my attention. The next day, another cold one in January, I was back on Pennsylvania Avenue, cheering the Clintons into town.
　　If that's not support and love, I don't know what is.
　　And prayers. During all the scandals, boy, was I praying. I won't say for what.
I'm not sure what inspiration I provided for Hillary. But I count three out of four as a good enough number to include myself in the sweeping dedication of her book.
　　So, why does it feel less than satisfying?

Perhaps trying to encompass approximately half the world in a book dedication is not a good idea. For one thing, someone is bound to feel left out. For another, and more important, why didn't Hillary cite her husband and daughter by name? After all, we all know who they are, and wouldn't it reinforce to them, her loved ones, that she actually remembers who they are?

Do I sound picky? Gosh, I hope not. Dedicating one's book is so personal, the one choice over which an author has absolute control through all the troubled waters of wrestling a manuscript between hard covers. Everyone from agents to editors to best friends offers his two cents' worth of advice and changes that must be made. Yet that dedication page rests there, clean and inviting, waiting for the author to lift a pen and immortalize – someone.

Think of J.D. Salinger's mom breaking open her pristine copy of *The Catcher in the Rye* and seeing: "To my Mother." Brings a tear to my eye. Mothers being what they are, she probably overlooked how Jerome actually portrayed them in print. Another truly interesting and personal dedication was Charles Lindbergh's when he finally got around to writing *The Spirit of St. Louis*, a quarter-century after his historic flight. His dedication: "To A.M.L. – who will never realize how much of this book she has written." That stirred up flurries of speculation at the time. Everyone knew Anne Morrow Lindbergh was the real writer in the family, and the word spread that she had ghosted her husband's memoir. But history has shown Lindy was as good a writer as he was a pilot.

Mary Oliver is a Pulitzer Prize-winning poet who suffered sorrows and abuse in adolescence. She now regularly publishes luminous volumes of verse, life-affirming and deeply in tune with the natural world, and every single book is dedicated exactly the same way – to her companion and life partner. It is comforting to pick up Oliver's most recent book and read, yet again, "To Molly Malone Cook." I know then they are still together, and the world contains that modicum of order.

J.K. Rowling wrote a delightful note in her first Harry Potter book:

> *For Jessica, who loves stories, for Anne, who loved them too;*
> *and for Di, who heard this one first.*

The dedication tells a story in itself. There is something a little sad about Anne. Jessica is a stand-in for all the children who read about Harry, but Di is really special. How wonderful to be the first!

Surely one of the great dedications is F. Scott Fitzgerald's for *Tender Is the Night*. A hauntingly autobiographical novel, written over 10 tortured years of decline while he tried to hang onto his enormous talent, Fitzgerald honored Gerald and Sara Murphy, a truly original couple and generous friends to the troubled author. He wrote simply:

> *To Gerald and Sara – Many Fetes.*

In that elegant phrase, he conjured up perfumed nights of revelry along the French Riviera and laughter and living well. Fitzgerald always could say a lot in a few words.

I could go on and on. It's difficult to narrow the field among so many remarkable tributes. I marvel that authors are able to do this at all. I speak from experience when I say it is not easy to come up with just the right words or the right person. A few years ago when I finished my first novel, I became flustered and blocked, trying to choose the one person upon whom to bestow the laurels of dedication. Time passed, and as my various relationships changed, so did my thoughts of who would appear on that all-important dedication page. For me, it was the equivalent of an actor who plans for years his acceptance speech for the Oscars. Who deserves such public recognition?

Many people will never know how often they were on the list and then scratched out. I did not want to tell anyone, because I think a dedication should be a surprise, perhaps even cause one to blush with pride. And what to do with all the other friends and family who will be hurt and offended?

These days, the solution for many authors, even in works of fiction, is to compose pages and pages of acknowledgements for the also-rans, the ones without whom this work would never have been written, etc. It almost seems that modern books are assembled by a committee, the lists are so long.

I confess I am equally fascinated by acknowledgements. Just how many people does it take to produce a book of, say, 300 pages? It's a little like watching today's inflated movie credits scroll by. As the artistic unions have become more precise and demanding about whom has made a credit-worthy contribution, the length of credits has become stupefying. Every guy who delivers bagels to the set or walks the star's dog gets his name up in lights. My favorite credit is for the "stand-by painter," the person who rushes in between takes and touches up little nicks and scars in the furniture or on the walls. Ah, show business!

This is only to make the point that, in literature as well as cinema, if too many people are given credit, the message becomes diluted and pointless. A book dedication should be striking and pithy, slightly intriguing, straightforward and yet mysterious at the same time. In that regard, I nominate as the greatest – ever – Herman Melville's dedication of *Moby Dick* to Nathaniel Hawthorne.

The two men became friends one summer in the Berkshire hills of Massachusetts where Melville was struggling to make a small farm earn enough to support his large extended family. Every morning, he locked himself in a second floor room to gaze at a far mountain and imagine himself at sea. In the afternoons, he would meet Hawthorne at the property line to walk and discuss the deepest issues of life. At only 32, Melville was in awe of the more established author and craving validation. When he finished his behemoth of a novel, the dedication page read:

In token of my admiration for his genius, this book is inscribed to Nathaniel Hawthorne.

Wow! The words stand there as if carved in granite, expressing a moment of friendship, of creation and of genuine love. There is nothing more to say.

Except, thanks, Hillary, for thinking of me, but here is a piece of advice: Next time – and, given the arc of your career and the success of your book, I'm certain there will be a next time – skip the generalities. Make it personal. Make it sing!

This year's Book Festival a best-seller
October 21, 2003

In the three years since its beginning, just a few weeks after September 11, 2001, the National Book Festival has risen in stature to rival the Kennedy Center Honors in celebrating and distinguishing excellence in American culture. Both events pay tribute to their honorees by inviting them to Washington for a weekend of parties at the White House and a gala, culminating in a series of elegant performances.

The Kennedy Center occasion takes place in the Opera House and includes only selected participants. The Book Festival, however, sits on the national Mall and invites the general public to meet 80 authors, poets, illustrators and storytellers and share in the wealth of their individual contributions to American arts.
First Lady Laura Bush welcomed the honored guests to this year's festival in the East Room of the White House, speaking of the

"power of books to bring us together." Indeed, that room gathered well-known biographers such as Walter Isaacson and David Maraniss, together with popular mystery writer Catherine Coulter and literary novelists Wally Lamb and Sue Monk Kidd. Basketball legend and author Bob Lanier, who leads the NBA's "Read to Achieve" program for children, presented the first lady with an all-star jersey for her efforts.

In her remarks, Mrs. Bush struck a note of commonality – how we all love good stories. "The story of our nation is a good story," she said, "pieced together like a quilt."

James Billington, the Librarian of Congress, a position he has held for 16 years, shared the podium. The Library sponsors and hosts the festival, although Mrs. Bush is a guiding force in its continuing success.

When asked to comment on the festival's future beyond the tenure of Mrs. Bush, Billington told me that it is "hard to predict, but the Library of Congress may go forward," in sponsoring the event.

Billington said the festival "fills a national need," and every year has "gathered momentum and added new elements." This year, the new elements included the Poetry and Home and Family pavilions. "More and more new homes are building libraries," he said, and spoke of the explosion in publishing of books on design, gardening and cooking.

The Library of Congress engaged in 3 billion transactions in 2002. Billington noted that the variety of the printed word increases by 6 or 7 percent a year. He sees the festival as an opportunity to celebrate that expansion and applaud the great diversity of American authors, in particular the diversity across generational lines. He said he thinks reading and the "physical presence of books – not just school assignments" are sources of success for many people he has known.

Recently, Billington accompanied Mrs. Bush to Russia for its own first-ever book festival. Asked if that festival was similar to ours, he explained it was for school librarians and involved individual projects. Nevertheless, "They were thrilled to see our first lady," he said.

What makes our National Book Festival thrilling and delightful fun is the presence of celebrities and television personalities among the highly respected, yet perhaps less universally visible, writers. Actress Julie Andrews, now a children's author, conducted a news conference with very young journalists, and Paige Davis and Frank Bielec, from The Learning Channel's television program, "Trading Spaces," traded jokes, promoted their books and demonstrated how to make fake tulle bows that will not wilt in humidity. During their presentations, the pavilions overflowed with eager spectators.

Certainly, though, all the pavilions were SRO for most of the day. Even as the afternoon waned, good crowds lingered in the poetry tent, absorbed in listening to Indonesian-born Chinese poet Li-young Lee and Kay Ryan, a poet whose brevity is mesmerizing.

If there is any fault with this event, it might be there is so much going on. In addition to reading and speaking, each author signs books and interacts with fans for an hour. One could go a little crazy trying to do it all – to hear and meet all the authors. How to choose between Juan Williams in History and Biography and James Patterson in Mysteries and Thrillers? Should I stand in line for Pat Conroy, or Anita Shreve, or R.L. Stine? Although selection and sampling are imperatives, for book lovers, these are pleasant dilemmas.

The one genuine problem I noticed this year – an almost comical one – was in the sales tent. Lines to buy books were slow and clogged. The book displays were difficult to peruse, and congestion was worse than Washington's Beltway at rush hour.

Even so, this drove home the point that commerce is not this festival's focus. Various corporations do sponsor parts of the event, yet their presence is unobtrusive. The heart of the day was the lively interaction between some of our country's most active, prolific and popular writers and their devoted readers.

Each year, the numbers attending the festival have grown, proving Billington's statements about momentum and expansion. I watched thousands of happy faces in the throng, heading for the Metro and staggering under the weight of satchels filled with newfound treasure. Surely, the National Book Festival is now a Washington institution and will continue, appearing in our city as regularly as the opening day of the Supreme Court, the first weekend in October.

Religion still propels best-sellers
November 28, 2003

Recently, the *Guinness Book of World Records* announced it had passed the 100-million mark in sales. That is quite an achievement, especially for a book that has been published only since 1955 and annually only since 1964.

Immediately, those who keep track of such things began calculating how the Guinness sales figures compared to the venerable best-selling book of all time, the Bible. The truth is, according to Russell Ash, who compiles lists in *The Top 10 of Everything*, no one "really knows how many copies of the Bible have been printed, sold or distributed." When one takes into account all of the translations and worldwide sales since the early 19th century, when publication figures began to be somewhat accurate, a number close to 6 billion is about as precise as it can get.

Still, the Guinness feat comes close to a tie for its time period of the late 20th century. Does this mean God is in a slump or tapering off as a prime subject?

Hardly. If current best-seller lists are any indicators, customers are eagerly seeking all sorts of reading matter on religion and spirituality. In fact, the hottest novel this year has been *The Da Vinci Code* by Dan Brown.

Brown has written a literate thriller compiled of rather arcane theological arguments that have existed since the writing of the Gospels. His plot boils along on the backs of a hunky Harvard symbologist and a French dish named Sophie. A tantalizing mixture of history, art, music and science teases the reader with the question of whether Jesus had a "personal relationship" with Mary Magdalene. Brown makes a search for the true Holy Grail seem like a breathless and current mystery.

Perhaps it is unfair to compare today's darling of the publishing world to yesterday's has-been. Yet not so long ago, David Guterson basked in the limelight with his stunning *Snow Falling on Cedars*, a deserved triumph. His latest, *Our Lady of the Forest*, left me wondering if fame and early success had driven the writer right off a cliff.

In his present effort, Guterson chronicles the tale of Ann Holmes, a scraggly teenage girl running away from an abusive stepfather and indifferent mother. She winds up in a crummy trailer park in the upper Northwest and supports herself by selling mushrooms that she gathers every day in the deep, deep woods. Her other main activity is what used to be called, euphemistically, "pleasuring oneself." Sickly and pale, she does not bathe or brush her teeth and is about as skinny as a nail, yet she inspires lust in just about every male who comes within a hundred yards of her.

One fine day, while going about her usual routine, a vision of the Virgin Mary appears to her in the forest, telling her to build a church on that very spot. The apparition tells Ann that she will appear for five days. As word of the miracle spreads through the Internet, drawing thousands of pilgrims to the forest, Ann goes to the young local priest and begs him to help her get started building Our Lady's church. Father Collins has a problem, though. He just cannot seem to focus on anything but his intense desire for Ann's increasingly ill body. If readers have not been quite repulsed enough by all the recent publicity about priests, the father's icky, prurient fantasies should finish them off.

Cutting to the chase, Ann is exploited by a shrewd con artist and fellow trailer park resident, she is stalked by a loser out-of-work logger who badly needs a miracle and, ultimately, she is the sacrifice everyone requires in order to fulfill their thoroughly despicable goals. Miracles, it is clear, are big moneymakers, and many people profit off her.

Judging from the charts, on which *Code* has stayed at the top for almost 40 weeks, and *Lady* has appeared not at all, religious themes sell well if they respect the reader and deliver a great story. Novels that exploit their subject, characters and readers will sink and disappear, even if an author possesses stellar writing craft.

(*The Da Vinci Code* by Dan Brown. Doubleday, 2003. 454 pages. *Our Lady of the Forest* by David Guterson. Vintage, 2003. 336 pages)

PUBLISHER'S NOTE:

Mountain Lake Press proudly released Jessie Thorpe's beautiful, haunting novel in 2020. It is available as an ebook, in paperback, as a hardcover edition and, as planned, soon to be an audio book.

www.ingramcontent.com/pod-product-compliance
Lightning Source LLC
LaVergne TN
LVHW011418080426
835512LV00005B/122